The Victorious Vagina

The Victorious Vagina

HOW TO BEAT A PLAYER AT HIS GAME

&

WIN AT SELF-LOVE

He says he's separated from his wife, so I believe that means they're heading to divorce. But, as a married male friend explains from a cheater's mind, "As long as she's not technically there at the moment, they are separated".

By

Katie Slade

Contents

Dedication

This book is dedicated to Josue Colin Yanez, his encouragement, friendship and commitment to this project made it come to life. And to my dearest friends, a few of you are in the book, and those that are not, I thank you for all your support.

Preface

Hi there amazing woman! I'm so glad you decided to check out my book, thank you.

"The Victorious Vagina" is a book, a true story containing a series of poems that chronicle the emotions & events that occurred when I was being courted by the man of my dreams. I was so deeply affected by what transpired between us, that I had to share my experience. I hope that my work inspires women to REALLY take their time getting to know a guy before deciding to become intimate with him.

Guys use love language to get sex, and we women use sex to get love. A key element as to why things are so f*d up in dating today. There's a famous old song, "Love & Marriage" go together like a horse & carriage, you can't have one without the other".

Back in the day, that's how it was. Fast forward to today, and while people still marry for love, there's a whole other group that's all about the hook-up & casual sex. The term "casual sex" couldn't be more perfect, people treat sex today like shaking hands. This sacred, beautiful, intimate act has been reduced to "a conquest", "something to do", "an ego booster".

Years ago an agenda was launched to delude women into believing that it was alright to have sex before marriage. To be as free as men to enjoy the carnal act of sex.

Problem is, we're not men. Just basic differences in our genitalia make it obvious.

A man can get aroused if the wind blows a in certain direction, not the case with we women. Our vaginas are like the little Russian Dolls, a layer, in a layer in another layer.

No wonder women have so much of a disadvantage climaxing! A friend once told me, she read, I'm not sure of her source, that when a woman orgasms with a man, her emotional attachment to him grows. And here's a fact, a woman is much more likely to get pregnant when she orgasms during sex. And why did God design us like this? To protect the very place life is conceived. A warm, cozy cocoon with just the right amount of moisture. That's why men are obsessed with getting back in there!

One last thing about the sacredness of sex, if it isn't an act that should be recognized as truly something exceptional & private, why is it illegal to have sex in public, practically everywhere in the world?! Why is the act of rape considered to be such a heinous crime? Because God gave us the ability to be intimate to share in loving & committed passion when procreating.

Many guys have mastered the art of seduction by using certain words & maneuvers.

They say the most flattering things, "you're so beautiful", "so smart", "I can't believe some one hasn't swept you up", "you swear you're not married, cause you're too hot to be single, let me take you to dinner, how about a weekend getaway at my South Beach condo...blah, blah, blah. They will say anything to get you into bed. We've all fallen for that one line or the promise that there will be more dates to come, thinking he seems really genuine. We fall for the bait, then, it's wham bam thank you ma'am. We've all been there, when that empty feeling hits you when he doesn't call after that night/moment of wild passion. When you felt the earth move, he said he felt it too, so why hasn't he called?! Well, in his defense, the earth was moving when he said it, you just let yourself fall in….so have I, sometimes in the deepest end of the pool!

My muse for "The Victorious Vagina" actually told me on our first date, that he had been praying to God day & night to send him a classy, smart & gorgeous woman, and Shazam there I was! Boy, he had me on Cloud 99! And, he treated me like a living goddess! Trust me when I say, I fell hook, line & sinker! I was not expecting this, I had been on a major man hiatus for several years. I had two horrendous back to back breaks up, my body, heart &

soul all needed a break from men. But, with him….I totally extinguished my firewall!!!

Prior to each poem, I'll share more details about what exactly was happening in our daily communications at that given point. This dating rollercoaster ride was unlike anything I had ever experienced.

Feelings of elation, patiently understanding broken dates, navigating miscommunications & the excitement of high-ticket adventures, all the while feeling, was this too good to be true? As women, we are too often ready to dive into the opportunity of a new & thrilling relationship. Guys know this, so they set up a picture perfect pool of passion & promises that send us jumping heart first, head second, right into our deepest desires.

So, without further ado, I look forward to sharing the intricacies & details of this chapter of my life. I pray you will enjoy reading, and learn how to avoid losing yourself in a relationship & how to fall in love with yourself. Whether Mr. Right shows up or not, we have to learn how to love ourselves more.

With sisterly love & peace,

Katie

Chapter 1: The Seduction

It was a hectic day at work. But, things were under control, as I organized & prioritized my tasks.

"Good morning Sunshine!"

He walked into the reception area, looking like a GQ model, perfectly groomed, close cut beard, skin the color of buttered toffee. He was bald, but his perfectly shaped, shaved head and glowing skin made him gorgeous even without hair. His hands were perfectly manicured, he wore cool guy jewelry, he really had style. Sporting a camel colored top coat with a luxurious cashmere scarf, he was beyond handsome, and his air of confidence was as enticing as his fragrance. I asked his name and who he had arrived to meet with. I contacted my colleague & asked him to sit for a few minutes.

He chose to stand & chat with me. I multitasked as we conversed, he complimented my efficiency. I thanked him, and expressed I was not well compensated for my experience & was in the process of interviewing.

"In that case, it would be super to exchange info. I've enjoyed our chat & I'd love to continue over coffee or wine."

I did my best to contain my excitement, when a huge pile of mail slipped off my desk and cascaded at my feet!

"I'm so sorry, let me help you!"

"You're very kind, but I can manage." I gave him my card just as my colleague arrived to meet him.

"To be continued," he said as he waved good-bye.

Just then a pretty red haired E.A. came whipping around the corner of my desk.

"Katie, who was that major hottie?!"

Obviously, I wasn't the only one who noticed how gorgeous he was, however, I was the one with his number! Score! A few moments later my my phone chimed, text message from Mr. GQ.

"If you're free for brunch Saturday or Sunday, I'd love to take you to a beautiful lakeside restaurant." Oh man, I already had plans with girlfriends. I was hosting a tree trimming party at my place, so no breaking those plans. Besides, better to not be too available right?! I told him I had plans, but how about the following Friday. He said he was having dental surgery

Wednesday and had no idea how he would be feeling by Friday. "If you have any time between now and Wednesday I'd love to see you." We made a plan for Monday after work.

I could hardly contain my exuberance! It had been ages since I had a date, never mind with a successful hottie!!! As I shared details with one of my best friends, Lori, she was brimming with glee for me.

"Whadda gonna wear?" Her Queens accent still cracked me up.

"A classic wrap dress with high boots. It's winter, I'll look chic & a little sexy."

That afternoon he texted to confirm and sent me the link to the restaurant he had chosen. A lovely place, but primarily communal tables. He asked my thoughts, when I mentioned my concern about privacy while chatting close to others, he agreed and asked what my fav spot was. His thoughtfulness was very touching. It was Christmastime and the places I offered as suggestions were completely booked, so we stuck with the original plan.

He picked me up promptly at 6:00. Looking deliciously dashing, he took my arm and escorted me to his latest edition, luxury white Mercedes Benz….can we say riding in style! The restaurant was lovely and very quiet. We were seated at a private table and shook off the cold night air. Equally excited to be in each other's company, we bantered blissfully about our lives. He was devoting his life to God & Jesus, just like me! A hottie, sexy, clever, a self made business owner with a benevolent business mindset. He was checking all the boxes.

The waitress poured an excellent Chardonnay, Mr. GQ was a lover of fine wine like myself. We toasted to a wonderful evening. He told me about his very difficult life growing up in the Caribbean, another connection we shared. Our conversation was a perfect volley of our life experiences, from work, to family, to relationships. His marital status was "Separated" for many years. Too many financial headaches to navigate kept them too entwined to get legally untwisted. He had his own place and loved living alone.

Wow! How many more things would we have in sync, living alone was a no brainer for me, I'd been living alone since I was 19.

Dinner arrived, he ordered more than enough, and at one point he was feeding me a delicious forkful of pasta.

"Isn't it excellent? I'm so glad you love to eat, we're going to have so much fun checking out places together!" He was staring at me, "What? Is everything okay? Are you having a good time?"

Smiling, I said, "I'm having an amazing time, and I'm looking forward to that too."

He drove me home, once parked, he said, "I have a surprise for you."

He pulled out a lovely bouquet of flowers from his back seat.

"I remembered how much you said you love flowers, I hope you like them."

"I'm speechless, thank you."

Our eyes met and we kissed, a long deep passionate & wet kiss! Wow! I'm a firm believer that a great kisser is usually a great lover! We slowly stopped, gazed at each other and said "Wow" simultaneously. We laughed and kissed some more. I was melting and it was getting late, there was work in the morning. He walked me to my door and promised to text when he got home. I stepped into my apartment grinning from ear to ear. I swooped up my adorable Yorkie and gave her a big kiss!

"Lulu, he's a winner!"

Through out the week I received morning calls and texts wishing me a wonderful day & reminders of God

& Jesus' love for us. I loved this, I had never had a man so comfortable and confident about his spirituality. He expressed while he was extremely busy with year-end projects, he couldn't wait to see me again. Our connection prompted this composition:

In the Midst of Your Presence" By Katie Slade

I want to bask in your light,

Your energy is so positive, so right.

I feel your strength, your power

I want to be with you hour after hour.

Your presence is a God given present

That makes me feel alive,

Makes me more resilient.

To the pressures and pains of life.

I've heard your story of your struggles and strife.

How you put God & Jesus first

Just as I do, because They quench our souls thirst.

You're a man of significant means

But you got there by Being on your knees

Praying to God & Jesus to help you on your way

To go out into the world and slay baby slay!

You've shared with me a faith filled vision

To get my life on a course of precision

By staying focused on the Source

Through life's obstacle course.

I thank you and applaud you

For all the good you've done,

And just knowing you has

Made me feel like I've won

Lifc's biggest love prize

When I gaze into your eyes.

Days turned into more than a week. Mr. GQ was constantly on my mind. I tried to keep my thoughts balanced, but he made it super hard. The sweetest morning and evening calls, random spiritual texts during the day. Our mutual requests for photos, fanned the flames of our flirtation, as we exchanged our hottest selfies. I felt like a teen again, sharing every detail with my girlfriends. One day I received a call on my cell, while I didn't recognize the number, something told me to answer.

"Hello?"

"Hola, it's Cattie?"

"Ahhh, si it's Katie."

"Que bueno jai have delivery for you."

In moments a floral delivery man was at my desk with a bouquet of exquisite red & white roses. The card simply said, "Thinking of You"! I tipped the delivery man and immediately took a photo. I texted, "You know your way to a girl's heart"! His response,

"I know how to treat a goddess".

Plans were made for a Saturday at the lakeside brunch spot that was his original first date plan. I was beyond thrilled at the thought of seeing him again. I was truly smitten! I could not think of the last time I had been this elated to be seeing a guy. My last two relationships had started hot, but turned into explosions of fiery fury that found me fleeing for my sanity and safety. My guard had been up for a couple years. So it felt wonderful to relax into a romance.

Friday night, I got my nails done and I planned an outfit, daytime fun & flirty. Sipping wine I imagined what a wonderful day we would have, the weather was forecasted to be cold, but bright and sunny. Saturday morning sun came beaming through my bedroom windows and I smiled at the thought of my day with Mr. GQ. After my prayers I turned on my phone. Three text messages from him: "Good morning Sunshine! Hope you slept well. I have an emergency, one of my workers was injured on a job site. I need to go to the hospital to meet his wife. Not sure about brunch, I'll keep you posted." Oh wow, I was disappointed, but felt bad that he was going to have to deal with this, and probably a workers compensation claim. Moments later I received text photos of his injured employee, pretty bad accident, TMI. But, I realized he wanted me to be aware of the severity of the situation.

I busied myself with weekend chores trying to keep my mind off the phone and the time. I knew the later it got the chances of us having our scenic Saturday brunch were slimming. He sent me an update, "Still at the hospital, not looking good for us, but my guy will be okay". My heart sank. Of course, I was happy his employee would be fine, but my feelings of excitement were deflated. Not wanting to appear spoiled & disappointed, I responded, "If you were coming home to me after a day like this, I'd have a chilled glass of wine waiting, with a steaming bath and a deep massage before dinner."

His reply, "Wow, baby that is the most beautiful & caring message I have ever received!

You're amazing, I'm going to make this up to you, I promise"! I smiled knowing how much I touched his heart. I knew he had football with friends on Sunday, so I didn't expect to hear from him.

First thing Monday morning, text… "Good morning Gorgeous! How are you?" Happy to receive his text, I replied doing fine getting ready for work. He wishes me a great day, shares bits about his hectic day and tells me he misses me….awww! Day in and day out, I receive the sweetest texts, like old fashion love notes, and I love that he's such a romantic. During a phone call one day he asks if I like basketball, I tell him, yes, one of the few jock sports I like. He says great, I'm taking you to the Barclays Center to see the Knicks. I say, it sounds great, but I can't do the nosebleed seats, they're downright scary. He says, "No Baby, we'll be VIP court side". He texts a photo of the VIP Lounge and comments, "We're all set with the tickets."

"Amazing, sounds good to me!" I replied.

It's now Christmas week, and I'm making plans to help my mom cook and take care of last minute gift items. It is truly my favorite time of the year! I love finding great gifts for family and friends and everything is so beautiful and festive. Mr. GQ continued to be very communicative. While he wasn't big on Christmas, sad childhood memories kept him from embracing the season. It was then that he told me about his challenging relationship with his mother. She never raised him and his brothers, she basically abandoned them. But, when he became successful, she was all about knowing her son.

"She wants for nothing, I take care of all her bills, cell phone, car payment, everything, and it's still not enough!" He stated with annoyance.

I shared some details of my mother's behavior toward me that was extremely hurtful. I could tell he was seriously scarred by his mother's abandonment. It was a "red flag" that I chose to see as "pink" because let's face it, we all have parent issues, right? I had some pretty intense issues with my mom.

Anyway, we brought the convo back to happier thoughts. He loved my girlish excitement for the holiday. He made it a point to let me know he had a gift for me.

"You do? You didn't have to!"

I realized how stupid that sounded, of course he didn't, but obviously he wanted to.

"I see how much you love Christmas, how could I not."

"Well, you're beginning to spoil me, and I like it!"

We both laughed, I thought to myself, this could be the best Christmas I've had in years, thank you God & Jesus! I was literally feeling like Mr. GQ was my Christmas gift from

God! We chatted for a few more minutes.

"What are your plans for Christmas Eve?" He asked.

"Well, surprisingly the office will be closed. I have an appointment with the vet for Lulu at 1:00, other than that I'm free."

"I'll be in your area dropping off some food and a donation at a church I support near your place. Can, come by for a little while and give you your gift?"

"Sure honey, that works, so looking forward to seeing you again, it feels like forever."

"I agree, can't wait for you to see your gift, I believe you're going to love it!"

As I return home from the vet with Lulu, I see his white Benz parked in front of my place. As he sees me, he exits the car with several bags. We both smile from ear to ear, and hug deeply.

"How are you Darling? Perfect timing. This is Lulu, my Yorkie."

"She's adorable! Hi Lulu, your mom told me about you & how pretty you are!"

Lulu immediately jumped to give him a kiss and proceeded to do her little rodeo dance

of excitement.

"I think she likes me! A good sign right?"

I agreed enthusiastically. If a dog doesn't like a guy, it's going to be a problem. I mentally breathed a sigh of relief as we walked to the entrance.

"What a beautiful apartment you have!"

I resided in a prewar building in Harlem. It was a spacious one bedroom with a large eat in kitchen, pretty much unheard of in a New York City apartment. The original parquet

hardwood floors were a show stopper, people always asked how I kept them so perfect.

I loved decorating, I had painted the living room a rich Oriental red, my furniture was a collection of vintage, antiques and newer (assembly required) catalog pieces, but all quality wood. Decorative pieces from my travels to various places around the world, were well displayed to remind me of how fortunate I was to have visited many amazing places. It was a warm and cozy abode that a friend once described, as sitting inside a beautiful jewelry box.

"I'm not surprised, he continued, you carry yourself with such class. And, I love the way it smells in here."

I was grinning widely.

"What's up?" he said.

"One of my exs could not tolerate any kinds of scented candles or oils, which I love. It was one of those annoying differences that I had to live with whenever he visited".

"Well, as I told you on our date, I love a quality scent candle".

Excellent, I thought, because that's exactly what I got you for Christmas. I took his coat and he unloaded the bags. He had brought several bottles of Chardonnay, more flowers and 2 beautifully wrapped gifts. As he placed the gifts on the coffee table, I took the wine and flowers to the kitchen.

"Would you like a glass of wine honey?" I called from the kitchen.

"Sure, thanks but not too much, I still have to drive." I brought two glasses of wine into the living room.

Lulu was jumping all over Mr.GQ and he seemed

to be really enjoying her attention.

She was trying to kiss him and he was giggling like a little boy, my heart was melting, it was an adorable sight. As he laughed and tried to catch his breath, I sat next to them.

As I pried Lulu off of him, I said, "It's my turn for kisses little flirt!"

Mr. GQ laughed, "I haven't had this much attention in forever!"

We both laughed. I handed him a glass and we toasted to "us" and a great year ahead.

"How has your day been?"

He replied, "Busy, delivering Christmas gifts to clients & the church, as I mentioned earlier."

"You are so incredibly giving, it really warms my heart."

"My grandmother really drilled into me to put God & Jesus first, she taught me the importance of giving. And, what you sow is what you reap."

"She was right, I like to say, Karma's a boomerang, what you put out, is what comes back."

"Wow, I like that, very clever!"

"Thank you an original "Sladeism", I like making

up sayings like, "She/He is shady as a palm tree!"

Mr. GQ chuckled. "Speaking of trees, your tree is beautiful, you and your friends did a great decorating job!"

I was enjoying him more and more, he wasn't your typical guy that took things for granted he really paid attention.

"Thank you Honey, we had a lot of fun!"

"Speaking of fun, he said, Let's open presents! By the way, I have one more gift for you, but it's not ready yet, the designer said by next week".

"Wow! I only got you one gift, you're too generous!"

"Baby, you didn't even have to get me anything, I just love to give."

He handed one of the gifts, "This one first."

I slowly unwrapped it to reveal a porcelain tree ornament of two little elves, their Christmas hats read "Katie" & "Lulu".

"Awwww, honey it's adorable! Thank you so much, it's going on the tree right now!" I gave him a big hug & kiss.

I found the perfect branch and hung it securely.

Settling back on the couch, he handed me the second gift. It was a small box in a little gift bag. "I really hope you like it." He sat on the edge of the couch watching me open the box with absolute excitement. When I opened the box I couldn't believe my eyes, it was the most stunning cross of diamonds set in white gold, I was speechless!

"Oh my goodness honey, it's gorgeous!!!"

"You really love it?!"

"I do, I do!"

He was beaming. "Let me put it on you. I picked it noticing that you only wear white gold or silver, and I got this length so you can always wear longer necklaces with it."

His generosity was overwhelming, I truly felt like I had FINALLY met the man God had destined for me.

I stared at us in the mirror, the cross hung perfectly at the base of my neck. I turned to face him, lovingly he cupped my face, kissed my forehead, the tip of my nose and then our lips met for the most delectable kiss! Oh my goodness, he was too delicious! Our tongues tickled each other, we sucked each other's lips, as our hands caressed our bodies. It was a long passion filled kiss that made me wet with desire for him. He guided me back to the sofa. We kissed more. As the moment became hotter, he pulled me on top of him, I could feel how aroused he was. He was hard as a rock and very well endowed. His button down shirt gave me easy access to his neck & chest. I kissed & licked his neck, flicking my tongue like butterfly wings, he moaned in ecstasy.

Slowly, he pulled my top out of my jeans and raising it up, he began to caress my breasts with strong, smooth hands.

Looking at my face, he said, "You are so stunning, I can't stop looking at you. And, your girls are so perfect & pert, I love them."

He took one in his mouth and began to tenderly nibble on my nipple, making my place of pleasure pulsate with drenching desire. I was proud of my breasts, while I was not voluptuous, they were more than a mouthful & pretty. We were swimming in a pool of passion, heading for the deep end when he said.

"Baby, can I have you? I want to please you so much."

I tittered on the very edge of temptation. I wanted him too! My mind swirled with images of our bodies entangled together, skin to skin, feeling the warmth of his powerful physique engulf every inch of me. Imagining the moment he would penetrate my pleasure palace. My vagina vibrated in anticipation. In those few seconds of contemplation, my head and heart took control of my lascivious libido.

"Darling, I want you too, so bad, but I think we should wait. You said you can only stay for a while, and I want us to be able to linger in the moment for as long as we like, without any obligations or time constraints."

With an obvious look of disappointment, he agreed.

"Of course I understand. He kissed me and ran his fingers through my long hair.

Everything about you is just perfect, I still can't believe I've met you."

My elation was beyond description, I literally felt like I was floating. We sat holding each other for a while wrapped in the warmth of our bodies. He kissed the top of my head.

"I've got to get going soon sweetheart."

I didn't want to move and I sure didn't want him to leave.

"I know you do my love. We got so carried away, you didn't open your gift."

I handed him his present, he opened it carefully

and with obvious anticipation.

"Hmmm, what did you get me, ahhh I know the luxury store you got this from, this is going to be special."

As he removed the top of the box the intoxicating aroma filled our noses.

"Wow! This candle smells amazing! It's so masculine & rich, I love it! Thank you so

much Baby, you have such great taste!"

"I'm thrilled that you love it! I know you enjoy your cigars, and one of the key notes is smoky tobacco. The burn time will last for hours."

"That's one of the things I'm really loving about you, you know the better things in life and you have such class!"

Man oh man, can this get any better? When was the last time I had someone who really acknowledged all that I brought to the table….uhhhh never.

Christmas morning was bright, the sky was cloudless. I spent extra time saying my prayers, counting all my blessings and asking God & Jesus to bless everyone in my life.

I had prepped the vegetables I was bringing to my mom's house, and all the gifts were neatly packed in a very large shopping bag. The phone rang, and I immediately saw it was Mr. GQ.

"Merry Christmas my love!" I gleefully answered.

"Good morning, good morning my beauty, Merry Christmas! How did you sleep?"

"Like I was floating on clouds! And you my love, did you rest well?"

"Yes, but I was up early. I spoke with my brothers and my mom's boyfriend, he started telling me how my mother cooked all kinds of food.

"For who?!!! I said. He's telling me for my brothers and me.

I was so mad Baby, I told him, she doesn't communicate anything. None of us knew she was cooking. I promised my Uncle Danny I would visit him and his wife. I also go to check on a very kind priest who runs a soup kitchen. But, my mother thinks of no one but herself."

"I'm so sorry to hear this Honey, I can only share that my mom has put me through some major changes too, she's been downright cruel at times!"

"Well, my mother turned her back on my brothers and me, basically she abandoned us.

I thank God for my Uncle Danny! I'm heading to

him now. What time are you going to
see your mom?"

"I'll head out around 1:00, dinner will be at 4:00. Would you like to join us?"

"Thanks Baby, but no, I need to see my brothers, so I'll go to my mother's later. But, text me from your mom's, maybe I can pick you up and drive you home."

"Okay, that's very sweet of you to offer. I'll touch base for sure."

As we ended our call I could feel his hurt over his mom's actions. Though he did his best to contain his emotions, he was seething with anger as he spoke about his childhood. I wondered if he had or would ever forgive her.

I arrived at my mom's as scheduled. My girlfriend, her mom, my sister and my adopted uncle were in attendance to celebrate. My mother's enthusiasm for Christmas had continuously waned over the years. She had less and less patience for the commercialization and the hectic pace that made usually normal people, run around like lunatics trying to accomplish everything before Christmas Day. I was on the opposite side, I loved Christmas for its true meaning, recognizing the birth of my Savior. Over the years my connection to God & Jesus had grown immensely, so I embraced Christmas to the max!

This ambivalent attitude of my mother's meant that I became responsible for all the prep, serving and cleaning up.

"Since you like to make a big deal of Christmas, you should be the one to orchestrate things," she stated.

As usual, her authoritative attitude had me moving at top speed to get dinner served as quickly as possible. She had sold her Brooklyn mansion and moved into a luxury apartment building. But, like many new apartment layouts, the kitchen left a lot to be desired. Limited counter space made it difficult to organize all the food being served. I found myself feeling overwhelmed. By the time dinner was served and devoured, I had completely forgotten to text Mr. GQ! Damn it!

I texted, "Hi Honey, are you still at your mom's?"

His response was, "Yes, but I'm feeling pretty tired."

I asked, "Do you still want to get together?"

"At this point, not really, I was waiting to hear from you. I'm going to head home shortly. I'll call you tomorrow."

I had so anticipated seeing him! His response left

me feeling sad and annoyed that I was so busy handling Christmas dinner, that I forgot to text him. Our little family gathering ended by exchanging gifts, requests for strong coffee with dessert and goodbye hugs & kisses. My sister drove Lulu and me home. Happy to be home, but unhappy Mr. GQ wasn't with me, I poured myself a little glass of an orange liquor and prepared for bed. I washed my face and stared at the sparkling cross that dangled around my neck. It was truly one of the most beautiful gifts I'd ever received. My girlfriends were floored at his generosity.

"Wow!, my longtime girlfriend Helen texted, "that's a very expensive gift, he hasn't even known you that long!"

I had sent her a photo of me wearing the cross. I agreed, but couldn't help feeling that maybe he truly felt I was his soulmate.

The next morning I received a text from Mr. GQ, it was Boxing Day, (recognized in the U.K. & the Caribbean as a day as important as Christmas), so he still had people to see & gifts to deliver. He'd call me later when he was done. He signed off with kisses & hugs. I smiled a cheerful smile and started my day. I connected with friends to catch up and share stories of our Christmas get-togethers. Most of us were single and lived far away from each other. We caught up on life, family gossip, workplace dramas and the latest dating sagas.

"Mr. GQ sounds like a dream, my dearest friend Freddy stated. I'm so happy for you Katie, if anyone deserves to meet a guy like this, it's you! You always give so much of yourself. You're gorgeous, kind, smart and funny as heck! He's blessed to have found you!"

"Oh Freddy, I adore you, thank you for your loving compliments!"

"They are all true and from my heart, after knowing you for years, it's about time you met a man that truly values you."

Freddy and I had met in L.A. years before and had become instant friends. He was my younger gay brother with a heart of gold, a sharp mind, loving positive spirit and an infectious laugh that made him a desired guest at every social gathering! Simply put, everybody loved Frederick! We ended our call with a promise of updates and more details about my evolving connection with Mr. GQ.

Christmas Day had landed midweek, so it was right back to work, the holiday spirit was already beginning to wane. I discovered that Mr. GQ was a very busy man all the time.

He woke at 4:00 every morning, started with a

HIIT workout, breakfast, shower and on the road by 5:30. Driving to various job sites to check on project development and resolve problems, by the end of the day he was toast.

Seeing him during the week would not happen, and he made it very clear that he was not into New Year's Eve.

"I was hoping that we could have dinner together at my place. I make excellent broiled lobster tails, I'll keep it simple with baked potatoes and broccoli with cheddar cheese sauce."

"Baby, that sounds amazing, but I'll be fasting and going to a spiritual retreat. I approach the New Year very differently than most people. I'm not into the club scene and all the craziness."

"Neither am I, I did all that stuff, I even did the whole Times Square ball dropping thing, never again I might add, it's all great till the ball drops then all hell breaks loose! I just enjoy having a few friends over, cooking, drinking and playing fun card games."

"Sounds nerdy!"

"Realllyyy?!" I replied.

"Just teasing you, sounds like a fun time, enjoy it my love."

We chatted aimlessly for a few more minutes and then he wished me sweet dreams.

He requested a bedtime selfie. It was only 7:30, and my evening was only half way through. Realizing he was heading to bed, I wondered if our lifestyles would mesh. I'm not a night owl, but I stayed up until at least 10:00. Our conversation left me feeling down. I thought for sure we would be together for New Year's, I was bummed. I sent him a sexy selfie of me on a beach in Ibiza, wearing a thong bikini. What a fabulous girls trip that had been! A classy photo that just might change his mind about New Year's.

Moments later I received his response text, "Where was this taken?"

Surprised by his question, I replied, "Last year in Ibiza, why?"

"You're wearing a cross that looks just like the one I gave you, I feel like an idiot."

"What?! I replied, "that piece is silver & cubic zirconia, no comparison to the real diamonds and pure gold of the cross you gave me." He didn't reply.

I decided to make a grilled cheese sandwich for dinner. Artisanal sliced bread, Gouda cheese, sliced tomatoes, gourmet fries and homemade coleslaw made the perfect sides. I poured a glass of my favorite

Chardonnay, put on some music and started cooking. I had taught myself to be extra good to myself when life threw me a curve ball or I got disappointed over a guy. I had experienced too many broken plans and promises, that left me feeling sad, depressed, and not wanting to eat. I vowed that I would never fall into the pity party place again.

I reminded myself of how blessed I was to, have my health, my own place, be gainfully employed and to be surrounded by loving friends & family. My dinner was the ultimate in comfort food, my grilled cheese had browned beautifully, the fries & coleslaw were perfect sides. I said grace and settled into my meal. Listening to excellent lounge music & reading a fabulous decor magazine, were perfect additions for a relaxing & much needed dinner.

The next morning I received a call from my recruiter, "They want to see you for a second interview! The women you met with think you're a great fit, when can I schedule you?"

I was bursting with exuberance. This was an awesome financial firm on Park Avenue.

The women I'd be working with were wonderful, the benefits were excellent and the salary was twice what I was making, I really wanted this position! I told my recruiter I'd make myself available for whatever time they wanted to meet.

"Super, I'll reach out to them and get back to you."

I couldn't wait to tell Mr. GQ, this would be a fantastic way to start the New Year for sure!

I arrived for my interview a few minutes early. It's always difficult to interview when you're employed. A concocted story of an important doctor's appointment was my explanation for a longer lunch break. Promising I'd be back as soon as possible, I left the office feeling confident with my fib and excited for my interview. This position would be a total game changer in my life.

Nicole, an executive assistant and the office manager, greeted me warmly and asked how I was enjoying the holiday season. She was wearing a gorgeous baby pink, cropped angora sweater with black leather leggings. I loved the look and loved that the office dress code was sophisticated chic. She reiterated the job responsibilities, shared again the upcoming company acquisition of another firm, that was causing the office to burst at the seams for more space, and the importance of being able to adapt to a quickly changing office environment. I assured her that I was ready to embrace all of the challenges. I had a successful meeting with two other executive assistants. As I departed Nicole asked when I could start, I wanted to say "tomorrow", but I professionally stated I'd respectfully give my current employer two weeks notice. I wished them all a wonderful New Year's and dashed back to my office.

I grabbed a salad as I walked back to the office. When I arrived there were a few fires to put out. My colleague and new friend, Malissa, did her best to handle the calls from frustrated tenants and vendors. The company had a notorious reputation for ignoring tenant issues and not paying vendors. This negligence often resulted in lawsuits and liens against the company. My position as the first voice of the firm, put me on the front line of these warlike situations. Angry callers caused a lot of stress. I used my diplomacy, patience and my gift of excellent communication, to shield me from the verbal attacks and threats. My dedicated demeanor did help to create some cease fires.

Later that afternoon I texted Mr. GQ with the positive results of my interview.

"I'm happy for you baby, but are you sure you want to leave? The job market is tough, a lot of firms are going under."

While I appreciated his concern, he had no idea the

hell I went through on a daily basis, and not being compensated nearly enough for my ability to go above and beyond my job description.

"Thanks darling but I don't think you really understand how toxic this environment can be. I'm tired of putting out fires I didn't start."

He expressed his sympathies and wished me the best of luck.

"By the way, please don't mention to anyone in the company that we are dating, I don't want anything to jeopardize what we have going on." It was a fair request, which I promised to honor. The next few days leading to New Year's were filled with usual excitement. I made plans to hang out with two girlfriends. One was single, the other was involved, but her guy was working, and I was in limbo. After all the romantic intensity that was flowing between Mr. GQ and me, I was feeling pretty down that we wouldn't be celebrating the new year together.

New Year's Eve arrived and I was in charge of bringing the champagne and my girls handled the snacks. We chatted about work issues, reality shows and how we all hated the coming winter! Watching the Times Square celebration on TV , we commented on the craziness of people willingly being barricaded, just to say they were there to see the ball drop.

I shared my experience of being 16 and going with my cousin and two guys friends to watch the ball and have a night of clubbing. The beginning was awesome, people shared champagne, laughed and told stories of how they traveled from distant cities to be there. But, once the ball dropped, it was every man & woman for themselves! People pushed & shoved fighting in opposite directions to get on with the rest of their night. I swore then, never again! We said our good nights at about 2:00 a.m.

I awoke fairly early, and I took the time to do some deep praying. I gave thanks for all my blessings, my family, friends, a save place to lay my head and excellent health. I thought of people by name and prayed for them individually. Being a very spiritual person, putting God & Jesus first in every aspect of my life made me feel grounded. I finished my prayers asking for success in my budding connection with Mr. GQ and that I would land the position I so wanted with the Park Avenue firm.

I spent the day cleaning and organizing things around the apartment. I texted a bunch of "Happy New Year's " to friends, and Mr. GQ of course. I wasn't expecting a reply from him, I knew he was at his retreat. In the late afternoon I prepared a wonderful bubble bath. Taking a relaxing bath was one of my favorite pastimes, I created a spa-like environment by lighting candles, playing soothing music & having an ice cold liter of water right at the side of the tub. I submerged myself in the hot and scented water, exhaling with delight. I luxuriated in my tub for over an hour, I had nodded off while meditating.

I was revived by the soft hum of my phone vibrating, a text from Mr. GQ. Short & sweet…."Happy New Year Baby! Hope to see you soon, I have one more gift for you, it wasn't ready for Christmas, remember? The designer just finished it. Have a great night,

I'll call you tomorrow."

I had forgotten that he had another gift, I was so taken with my cross! My mind was filled with curiosity, but more than that, my mind was filled with thoughts of seeing him again. I decided that in light of his extreme generosity, I'd get him another gift too.

The next day I was back at work, the holidays were a vague memory and reality was biting. Dark mornings, frigid temps and growing unhappiness at my place of employment, made me yearn for a fantasy escape from winter & life with Mr. GQ…..a girl can dream. During lunch, I went to the men's section at one of the upscale department stores. I selected a cool beaded men's bracelet that I knew would look super with his other pieces. I had it gift-wrapped and went back to work.

At the end of the day, I got a call from my recruiter. "Sorry Katie, they chose another candidate".

My heart sank, oh man, I wanted it so bad, I couldn't believe it!

"Unfortunately, they really need someone to start immediately, while you were their number one choice, your two weeks' notice to your current employer made their decision, they just couldn't wait for you. I'm working on a few other things, I'll keep you posted."

She hung up before I could say anything. I was feeling lower than an ant. I thought I had the job for sure, well I did, but by doing the right thing by my thankless employer, I screwed myself out of a great gig! No good deed goes unpunished….I hated that saying, true as it sometimes was.

When I got home Lulu was thrilled to see me as always, she did her little rodeo dance of excitement and it helped to wipe away the disappointment of the day. We had a quick walk, it was freezing and Lu was not a fan of the cold. I loved watching her little paws skip quickly on the ice cold pavement. It was impossible to keep booties on her paws, so she moved fast! She did her business and we were home. I undressed us both, poured a glass of wine and decided what to have for dinner. Being a consummate foodie, I was glad my mom had me cooking at a young age. As the child of a Jamaican woman, it was mandatory that my sister and I learn to cook. Scanning my refrigerator, I decided I'd make one of my fav meals, a recipe I snagged from a gourmet food chain. A mushroom and cheese quesadilla, with truffle fries and sautéed garlic spinach….my mouth salivated and my stomach growled.

I showered, put on a designer black velvet tracksuit, a gift to myself for all my hard work.

I lit candles, played music and started preparing dinner. Lulu was lounging in her second doggie bed close to the stove, watching my every move in case a morsel should fall from my cutting board. She was a foodie like her human mom, and loved to eat everything I ate. Lulu was truly God sent! She filled the unconditional love void. I had purchased her from a pet shop. While many advocated adopting a dog, the adopter must understand if they need to give love or get love. I was not in the mindset, at that time, to nurture an emotionally or physically abused dog. After two horrendous back to back break ups, I decided to take a major hiatus from men. I needed a pup that came with no baggage. I had been emotionally battered & bruised, chastised for my cellulite, talking too much, wanting to sleep in on weekends, taking too long to get ready, blah,blah,blah!

Twice I had fallen for really good looking guys. The first, a seemingly successful financial advisor. A Jewish man who was self described, as being more superstitious than religious. While he was respectful of my commitment to God & Jesus, he could not abide my wearing a cross or seeing my rosary. It was awkward, but I did my best to ignore the difference in our religious upbringings. He was the first born of a very bitter and unhappy marriage. He was a mama's boy. She doted on him and defended him at every turn in his life, which only led to his detriment. She even defended him to police during an arrest, when he was a teen and clearly in the wrong. This lunacy and lack of discipline, led him to believe he could do no wrong. As an adult, this mentality created a scenario of tyrannical tantrums when he didn't get his way. He used his good looks and sexual prowess, along with just enough cultural & street cred to make him appear to be a great catch.

However, after five long years, of his dangerous driving, flirtatious flings and maniacal meltdowns, I finally realized I could not undo the damage done by his doting mother. I couldn't change him, why do we women think we can change a man? So, in the end, I left him. I threw him back into the waters of wailing women to try their hand at reeling him in.

The second, was the first Black man I had ever dated. I was raised to not see color, but the caliber of the person. Sadly, many of the Black men I encountered, were married, gay or just not of my milieu. He appeared to be more on my level. He was a proud man that carried himself with an air of confidence, he dressed with an extreme attention to detail, and was one of the most handsome men I'd ever seen. Gainfully employed and a dedicated bodybuilder, he was financially responsible and had an impressive physique that made a girl feel protected. However, once again, the external package was a thick veneer that covered a tremendous amount of insecurity and unhappiness. Those issues caused him to doubt my faithfulness and created an insane desire to control me. This eventually led to him sneaking into my phone to dig for dirt, searching to find anything that he could use against me, and sabotage the relationship. His unscrupulous & illegal tactics led to an explosive end to our doomed relationship.

I thought about Mr. GQ, handsome and successful, but with some major mommy issues, was I falling for another man carrying emotional baggage? Only time would tell, at least there were no spiritual or jealousy issues to contend with this time around. The mental trip down memory lane made me even more hungry! I said my grace as always, and I settled into my delicious dinner, giving little nibbles to Lulu. It was Thursday morning, I did a big stretch, said my prayers, made my bed and got ready to walk Lulu.

One more day to the weekend, I had no plans for the weekend, but just knowing I'd have a break from the insane asylum I called my office, was a cheerful thought. Back in my apartment, I wiped Lu's paws, got her breakfast ready and prepared my morning tonic of fresh squeezed lemon, fresh grated ginger & turmeric, cayenne and aloe juice. I had stopped drinking coffee for years and felt all the better for giving it up.

I showered, listening to my favorite morning radio show. The music was all current and upbeat, but the best part of this show was a segment regarding being ghosted after a date. This was broadcasted in real time, a caller would share a dating scenario where they were ghosted for reasons unknown to them. The radio host would call the ghoster, while the ghosted stayed quietly on the line. A free date would be offered, but it had to be with the ghosted person, when the ghoster refused the date, the radio host would beg for an explanation.

This led to the most outrageous details, there had

been everything, from a bed wetting drunk guy, to a drunk girl who openly flirted with her date's brother, and then called the brother's name while they were having sex, to an octogenarian gent who couldn't keep his dentures in while making out with his date! I was constantly in hysterics or shaking my head in disbelief. These anecdotes were real, and most of the participants met via dating apps. Sometimes a second date would be agreed to, but most times it ended with the ghoster being pissed off and hanging up.

It was more than entertainment for me, it was an insight to the world of dating in the millennium. Some people still had strong morals and were unwilling to conform, others were self consumed and going through the motions with the hope that their soulmate would magically appear via an app. I wasn't one for online dating or dating apps. I had tried one of the popular sites years before, and after one week I gave up. The guys with attractive photos and nice bios, never responded, and the guys that were a 3 or 4 out of 10, that reckoned themselves an Adonis. As far as I was concerned, it was a total time waster and I got my money back.

I decided to wear a black cashmere turtleneck sweater, the diamonds in my cross sparkled beautifully around my neck, I still couldn't believe his generosity!

A grey pencil skirt and suede ankle booties completed my outfit. I always went to work looking fashionable, and the owner of the company loved that I cared so much about my appearance. I had been awarded the "best dressed" prize in the office earlier in the year. I bundled up in my fur, kissed Lu, left classical music on for her and headed for the subway.

When I got to the office, things were fairly quiet. I handled a few tasks that had been left on my desk. Things were going smoothly, until I picked up my first irate call of the day. "Good morning The J.M. Group, how may I direct your call?"

"Yeah, I want to speak to the head of accounting or your legal department."

Oh boy here we go. "May I ask what this is regarding?"

"Sure, your company is calling for HVAC service, but you guys owe us $173,433.62, there is no way we can provide any service until this is paid, and right now two of your residential properties need boiler repairs."

Another example of how poorly managed this company was! I transferred him to the head of residential properties. In two minutes he called back.

"Look, I don't want voicemail, want to speak to a person! You guys have been jerking us around for payment for months and I'm fed up! Now, get me someone to speak with or

I'm getting my attorney involved!"

I took a deep breath and counted to ten.

"Hello! Are you there?!"

I calmly answered, "Yes, I'm here sir. All I can do is present this information to the most senior people in the company. I will convey that if someone does not respond immediately, that you will be taking legal action." He grumbled a response and slammed the phone down in my ear!

I shook my head, thinking about how the owner of the firm lived an extremely lavish lifestyle, but he didn't think twice about his tenants potentially being without heat or hot water in the dead of winter. These situations kept me on the interviewing carousel. The rest of the day was busy with all kinds of administrative tasks. Colleagues came by to chat or complain. I had made a few close friends and our camaraderie definitely helped to lift the negative energy that enveloped the office. The day flew by and before I knew it, it was almost 6:00!

When I arrived home, I suited and scooped up Lu, it was frigid and I wanted her to do her business quickly. Mission accomplished, we were back in the warmth of my apartment in minutes. Undressed and drinking wine, I played with Lu before my shower.

She lived for "fetch & return" and I was happy to dedicate this time to her. She was alone all day and it was only right I give her as much attention as possible when I got home. Before making dinner I texted Mr. GQ, "Hi Honey, I hope your retreat is going well. Please touch base when you can, thinking of you!" I decided I'd wait to tell him about his extra gift voice to voice. I was super excited to give it to him.

Chapter 2: The Manipulation

Early Friday morning, I said my prayers, stretched, and did my morning routine.

Turning on my phone I got an automatic voice text notice from Mr. GQ. "Good morning

Gorgeous! How are you my love? I'm already on the road. I'm hoping I can see you tomorrow, I have to be in the city and I want to stop by and give you your gift. Let me know if that works. Have a beautiful day, big kisses." He sounded happy & full excitement, I guess the retreat really did him a world of good! And wow, he wanted to connect tomorrow! I had no plans and thought, "we can finally have a wonderful

Saturday night together….yay!!!" I quickly responded that I couldn't wait to see him. I was so glad I had gotten him the bracelet, I couldn't wait to give it to him, and show him that I was a giver too, and didn't take his generosity for granted.

The office never permitted the wearing of jeans, even on Fridays, so I decided on a pair of classy black cords with a white turtleneck, black blazer, designer scarf and black riding boots. I looked country club chic and of course my new diamond cross added just the right touch of bling!

"Happy Friday!" I greeted Mali with a big hug.

"Good morning Honey Bunny, happy Friday to you too! You look extra happy, what's up?"

Mali had become a trusted friend, I truly valued our connection, she had my back at every turn and I had hers. I had broken my promise with Mr. GQ and had told Mali about our dates, I knew I could trust her to not share with anyone else in the office.

"Looks like I'll finally be seeing Mr. GQ tomorrow night!"

"Look at your smile, you're beaming! You're really into him huh?"

"Girllll, I've never met anyone like him! He believes in God & Jesus, he's handsome, successful & very generous, he's almost too good to be true!"

"I'm soooo happy for you Katie, you so deserve to have a great guy."

"Thank you my Angel, you're too sweet."

I had purchased breakfast pastries for us, we nibbled as our day got under way. While I looked forward to Fridays with great anticipation, it was pizza day in the office, and that always was an added pain in the neck. Many employees were Jewish and only ate kosher, sadly the kosher pizza place left a lot to be desired. After months of complaints from the non Jews, the company finally agreed to order from a non kosher place as well.

So, in addition to ordering just the right number of pies, making compromises with the staff on toppings, I had to make sure the non Jews didn't eat the kosher pizza if it arrived first, and vice versa with the Jewish folks. Sound like a headache…it was! I breathed a sigh of relief once lunchtime was over.

The day ended quickly and I was on my way home. I had refrigerated my pizza slices and saved them for dinner, it was the easiest thing to do after a long week. Lulu, as usual, was thrilled to see me. We dashed out and dashed right back in. I cleaned her paws, gave her a treat and poured some wine. As I undressed I thought about tomorrow night with Mr. GQ. Just then my phone rang, it was him! It rang twice.

I answered, "Hello Darling, how are you?"

"Good evening Gorgeous, what are you up to?"

"Oh, just getting undressed after a long day, and thinking about you. How was the retreat?"

"Getting undressed, don't tell me these things, you

make me want to drive to you right now!"

I giggled, loving that I was such a source of temptation.

"Don't laugh, I'm serious. You had me ready to explode on Christmas Eve! Woman, you are one amazing kisser! You know, not everybody knows how to really kiss with passion….but you!!! Let me stop before I can't control myself!"

I was grinning from ear to ear and I could feel my private place getting very warm.

"Well, you definitely win a prize for best kisser, you had me going too y'know!"

We laughed together, and bantered on about our day. I told him I didn't get the job, and he expressed his sympathy.

"Well, at least I know just where to find you. Why don't you ask the big man for a raise, I know he sees how valuable you are to the company."

"It's just such an insane place to work, sometimes it's beyond the money, but I'll think about it. So, what brings you to the city tomorrow?"

He said he was going to see a building he wanted to buy. He was still negotiating with

the seller.

"I won't go above $10 mil, so we'll see what happens."

I'd never been involved with someone who played in these money arenas, so I was impressed. I told him how much I couldn't wait to see him, he felt the same.

"You've got another gift waiting for you too."

"Awww, Babe you didn't need to."

"I know, but you've been so thoughtful, and I wanted to. Can't wait for you to see it, it's something that will remind you of me all the time."

"Gorgeous and generous, how did I get so lucky, thank you God."

I melted. He told me he'd touch base tomorrow when he had a better idea of what was going on, I said for sure and we said our good nights with hugs & kisses.

Saturday morning, I awoke with a smile and thought this is going to be an awesome day! I said my prayers, did my usual routine, walked Lulu, and spent the morning changing the sheets, vacuuming and cleaning my place thoroughly for the arrival of Mr. GQ. I showered, washed my hair and as my hair air dried, I gave myself a pedicure. The cost of living in NYC and a low paying job, did not allow for luxuries like hair salon visits and mani / pedis. Once in a while I needed to see my Dominican hairdresser of 15 years, Olga. She did a fabulous job for the best price. But, I saved a lot of time and money doing my own pampering, and luckily I was good at it.

I dried and flat ironed my hair, it looked fabulous! At 1:00 I got a call from Mr. GQ, he was waiting for the seller. He expressed that he wasn't sure what time he'd be finished, but he'd keep me on his radar. I told him that I was ready to see him at any point. He said the feeling was mutual and he'd call me later. The anticipation of seeing him was driving me insane, I had to reel myself in and focus on me. I decided to start preparing my business tax receipts, a tedious task, but it would need to be done sooner or later.

The year before I had created an app called "My Girlfriends' Favorite Gifts." The concept was designed to help women gift each other with more personal and desired gifts. By completing a profile and sharing it with friends, gifting would be easy and a successful no brainer. It was even great for husbands & boyfriends. People thought it was a really terrific concept. I worked tirelessly with the developer designing the layout.

The crazy thing was I did not embrace technology, but it only made sense to accept the realization that everyone lived on their phones and apps were the future. Personally, I couldn't understand the preoccupation with cell phones. I saw my ex lose his mind when he misplaced or lost his phone, which happened ALL THE TIME!!! I had heard horror stories of phones getting stolen and the outrageous cost of replacing them. I was fine with my ever convenient flip phone.

Until one day I got a call from my app developer. The company was based in Atlanta and the staff were all locals. A man with a heavy southern drawl said,

"Hey Katie, I'm Jason, I'm going to be your blueprint designer for your app."

"Hi Jason, nice to meet you."

"Thanks Katie, nice to meet you too. So, Katie, how do you want your app released?"

I asked, "What do you mean Jason?"

"Well, do you want iOS or android?"

I said, "What's the difference?"

After a pause Jason said, "Well, Katie what kind of phone do you have now?"

"I have a flip phone."

The howl of laughter from the other end of the line made me feel like I had told the funniest joke in the world! Once he regained his composure, Jason said,

"Sorry Katie, you're going to have to get a real cell phone to be able to interface with your own app!"

That afternoon, I went from horse & buggy to a Ferrari, as I put my flip phone out to pasture, embraced my new cell phone, shocked my friends and entered the new millennium.

My foray into the app world was a baptism by fire! Initially, I was extremely excited to be endeavoring into an entrepreneurial enterprise. People loved the idea, a few millennials I had shared the concept with actually commented they wish they had thought of it. I loved being creative, and I began working consistently with the app developer's creative team. The staff was friendly and helpful. A few weeks into the process, I received a call from one of the owners of the app development company. His name was Damien, and he thought the concept of my app was brilliant. He expressed that unlike other apps, my app was being built around social interaction, not solo time with the cell phone. I was so thrilled to be hearing this from an expert in the field, I was beyond excited with my new found venture! Damien wanted to give my app priority in its development to get it released as quickly as possible. When I asked what was needed from me to expedite the process, he said $5,000! Ouch! Reality was biting hard! Not expecting his response, my elation quickly evaporated when I realized the funding this was going to require!

I decided the investment would be worth it, one had to spend money to make money, was the mantra of business minded people. After months and months of collaboration, time, and constant dedication to the design and imagery, the app was finally coming to fruition. I completely embraced my entrepreneurial role and began marketing it to everyone I met. I remembered reviewing the UI files and thinking, when this takes off I can start to make residual income from something I created. One day I got an email from an Asian colleague, stating that she had blocked me from her message account.

Evidently, someone was pretending to be me, then revealed that they were actually my app developer trying to reach me. What?!!! This was insane! I promptly called my developers, and shared the bizarre details. The senior manager I spoke with said he would reach out to my project manager immediately. Oddly, she had become very unresponsive with me. He later informed me that she had resigned after being questioned about my account. That was the beginning of the end.

To make an agonizing story as short as possible, the company had experienced an internal sabotage. Two principles colluded to undermine the founder, farmed the coding out to Chinese coders for less money, ripping off clients like myself, and pocketing a ton of money. Damien was one of those principles, I knew his name meant trouble from day one. This was one of the biggest nightmares I had ever experienced, the $18,000 I had invested in the development had no value if I couldn't get the coding! I pleaded with the founder to please work with the Chinese to get whatever coding they had. He said he was trying, but it was like pulling teeth.

To make financial matters thousands of dollars worse, my accountant advised me that NONE of the $18,000 I had invested could be written off as a business expense until the app was up and running. I cried, I screamed and I thought I'd lose my mind!

"Why don't you sue those bastards?!" my mother demanded of me.

After much research, I found an honest arbitrator that told me to save my money and myself more aggravation.

"Ms. Slade, let me give it to you straight, their corporation was established in Dade County, Florida which would require you to fly here several times to attend the proceedings. And, even if you won in the end, if they don't have the money, you will be out of pocket for your attorney fees, travel expenses and maybe their attorney fees too.

Take whatever money you have and finish your app. I wish you well." I thanked him with all my heart for his time and honesty. God saved me from another major expense I couldn't afford. I called other app developers that suddenly appeared in searches that I never saw before. I discovered Damien's company had paid to be listed first on multiple platforms. These new developers felt sorry for me, but their costs without any coding was tens of thousands, which I didn't have. In the end, my accountant had a friend who was an entrepreneurial app developer.

Deen was a good guy. I showed him the UI files. His response, as we met at a chain coffee shop, was "Yup, this is like a $25,000 app."

He agreed to do it for $8,000 understanding my predicament and minimal funds. We worked well together. After more months of late night calls, working weekends and networking, the app was finally released. In the end, the cost of the updates, bug fixes and constant tech issues, I licked my war wounds and I archived the app. Nothing ventured, nothing gained. I suddenly realized it was almost 5:00 and no word from Mr. GQ. Hmmmm, I decided to text him.

"Hey Darling, how's it going? Any updates?"

About ten minutes later he texts, "Still in this meeting and I'm starving!"

I texted back, "Tell me what you want for dinner, I'll cook."

"No, no honey, I have no idea how much longer this will be."

"Well, do you still want to see me?"

"Of course I want to see you, and I have your gift. Let me touch base with you in a bit."

By 7:00, I still had not heard back from him. I was getting the feeling that this was going to be another broken Saturday plan. Feeling frustrated and hungry too, I called my girlfriend Lori.

"So, it's been well over a month and you've only seen him twice?! I think that's weird, especially the way he keeps telling you he wants to see you. I don't care how busy any guy is, if he really wants to see you he makes time! I smell a rat, I think he's still married!"

"No Lor, I'm sure he's just super busy! He's really successful and he's always on the go!

I know he wants to see me and he's been mentioning this other gift for days now."

My argument of defense for Mr. GQ was not convincing my longest friend.

"Look, I don't want to see you get hurt, you've been investing a lot of time thinking about him, and buying him stuff."

"I only bought the candle and bracelet."

"Yes, but your money has been tight. Just keep your guard up, you haven't dated in a few years and there are plenty of players out there. I got to go, Joe just came home and we're going out to eat. I wish we lived closer, I'd treat you to dinner. I love you, keep me posted."

When I hung up I felt sad and confused. Was Mr. GQ a player? Oh man, I hoped not, things were feeling so great. But, Lori was right, something wasn't kosher. Chardonnay to the rescue!

"Well Lu, looks like it's just you & me, all dolled up with nowhere to go." I lit one of my favorite scented candles to lift my mood. I put on a compilation cd of female R&B singers. Linguine & clam sauce with sautéed broccoli in olive oil and garlic was just what

I needed to put Mr. GQ out of my head. I watched

one of my favorite shows that combined food and travel, as I indulged in my dinner. This episode happened to be on Italy, a perfect pairing with my pasta! An hour later I had cleaned my plate and Lulu licked her chops after her final piece of a baguette with butter. I took the dishes to the kitchen, washed everything and left them to dry. 10:00 time for bed, and no word from Mr. GQ, he had some explaining to do.

Sunday morning, I relaxed in bed after my prayer session. I prayed for Mr. GQ hoping all was okay with him. And, I prayed he wasn't a player. Another freezing NYC day! I hated few things in life, winter was one of them! I hated being cold and I was not a fan of the snow or winter sports. I had not ice skated since I was a teen and I didn't ski. One year my mom took my sister and me to Lake Placid, a skiing trip I'll never forget.

Several women in my mom's office decided to book a ski trip to Lake Placid, New York.

The Winter Olympics had been held there years before. My mother decided this would be a fun excursion for the three of us, a weekend escape from the city, with people she knew. Excited as all get out, my sister and I couldn't wait to go shopping for our ski stuff.

At 13 and 15, we wanted the coolest and latest ski

gear, even though we had never skied before, we knew we had to look cool. When my mother saw the cost of the down ski jackets & pants, she had sticker shock!

She said "Okay, you'll each get a jacket, but no pants, you'll wear your long johns with jeans." Well, any skier knows, once you fall and get wet with jeans on, you're just miserable and cold! Frugal Frieda a.k.a. my mother, refused to buy chair lift tickets and insisted we'd be fine using the T bar lift. For those of you that are not familiar with the T-bar lift, this is an on the ground cable that comes by with the T bars hanging and you have to grab one as it's moving, with your poles under one arm as you grab the T bar with the other arm and it propels you forward up the slope. I slipped and couldn't get up and as I struggled to help myself T bars came by hitting me in the head!

My mom yelled, "Get up, I paid for these tickets, figure it out!"

Embarrassed as hell, I struggled to stand trying not to break my leg, as I uncrossed my skis! Of course the sight of me had people trying to hold back their laughter. Our gorgeous ski instructor stood shaking his head. Not one of my finer moments. As life would have it my sister won the prize for "Best Beginner." That was my first and last skiing experience.

At almost 2:00 I received a call from Mr. GQ.. "Well, if it isn't my favorite real estate

tycoon, how are you?"

"Oh Baby, I'm so sorry, the guy was being a real jerk! He got there super late, we had to tour the building, that took forever, but I had to inspect it."

"But, you never even called me."

"By the time we were finished I was so tired and so hungry I couldn't think, I'm sorry.

Don't you know how bad I want to see you and give you your gift?"

He romanced his way back into my heart again.

"So, how did you spend your Saturday," he asked with sincere interest.

"Doing my tax return prep."

I shared the story of my app endeavor. I wanted him to know that I was not a woman who was looking for a man to take care of her.

"Oh man Baby, that's quite a saga, I'm so sorry!"

"We live and we learn."

"Well, I'm proud of you seeing it all the way through, and you got it up and out there."

"Yes, that's true."

"So many people have ideas and never even try to execute them. At least you turned a dream into reality and that counts for a lot."

I really appreciated his compassion and how attentively he listened. As our conversation came to an end, he promised to make time during the week to see me, sending me big hugs and kisses.

Monday morning dread descended on me like a boulder. It was so cold, so dark, and was that sleet I heard hitting the window?! I pulled the covers up over my head. I really HATED winter. I thought to myself, "Why can't we be like bears and just hibernate through the winter months?!" The thought of calling out sick was a very enticing idea. I laid in the chilly darkness of my bedroom thinking about my life. I had to start thinking of another entrepreneurial endeavor, I was never going to rise to another financial level working a 9 to 5. I said my prayers giving thanks for all I had in my life. Guilt got the better of me, and I decided not to call out sick. I pulled my very warm robe up over my duvet and slipped in one arm at a time, doing my very best not to expose my body to the chill in the room. With a pillow over my head, I strategically reached for my lamp.

Clicking it on, I slowly moved the pillow down taking in the lamp light. My bedroom was the coldest room in the apartment. I had done my best to insulate the windows, but cold air still found its way through the cracks, a drawback to living in a prewar building.

I totally suffered from SAD, I was thankful to know that the disorder actually existed and people around the world suffered from it. It's always comforting to know you're not crazy or alone! One day I would live in a year round warm climate. Another reason I had to start making more money! Finally out of bed, my winter wake up process added an extra 15 minutes to my morning routine, and I always found myself running to the subway.

"Katie, can you please scan copies of these liens to the people on the post-it, thanks a lot." The request was from the general counsel of the company, Henry.

"Sure Henry, happy to help you."

He possessed a relaxed and easy going demeanor, a real contrast to several other company execs. I liked him, and he liked and valued me. Henry always said "thank you" which went very far in my book. A few members of the senior staff were snide, condescending and completely unappreciative. Henry relied on me often since his assistant, Mara, had quit months before. She felt overworked, underpaid, and she had a very hard time working with the assistant general counsel, named Alan. He was younger than Henry, and had a pompous and demanding attitude.

Months back, Mara had come to my desk a nervous wreck. Apparently, a UPS overnight envelope had arrived for Alan, and I had signed for it, but neither she nor Alan had it.

"Do you remember seeing it or signing for it? she asked, trembling. The bank called

Alan and said the document is time sensitive, now he's angry and blaming me."

"Okay, take a deep breath. Please provide me with details, you know if something is addressed to Alan, I give it to you or directly to him."

"I know you do. Will you please come to his office with me?"

"Alright, let's go." I said with irritation over the situation.

We stood at the threshold of Alan's office door. He sat staring at his computer like we weren't there. I tapped lightly on the door.

"Yeah, what's up?" he said with his usual attitude.

"I'm here to help Mara get to the bottom of locating this time sensitive document sent to your attention."

"It wasn't sent to my attention, it was just sent to J.M. Group."

"Well, can you provide me with the sender's information, so I can try to search my memory and retrace my steps?!"

I was professional, but indignant as I made the request. I was very on top of my job, and rarely made errors of this nature. Besides, I was not going to cower to his arrogant and demanding personae.

Alan turned his computer monitor in my direction, forcing me to step into his office.

"That's the bank that sent it, and that's the entity it's regarding." He stated with aggravation.

As I looked at the copy of the air-bill, it seemed familiar, but I honestly handled so many overnight envelopes it wasn't ringing a specific bell in my mind.

"Well, it's going to take me a bit to track it down. I have other issues pending."

"I don't care, just find it!" came his biting response.

Mara and I walked back to my desk. I shook my head in annoyance.

"I don't know how you work with him, does he think we just lose stuff on purpose!"

Mara's eyes brimmed with tears, as she explained that this document was necessary to complete a closing on a $50 million dollar deal. Great! I thought, just what I needed to hear.

I checked with the property manager of the entity, no luck. Then remembering it was sent by a bank, I checked with the property accountant.

"Hey Dave, did I give you an overnight envelope for this bank?" showing him a copy of the air bill.

"No, I don't think so," he replied.

Dave was not the sharpest tool in the shed, so I took it a upon myself to search the pile of mail on his desk, sure enough, there it was! When I returned to my desk I called Mara and told her I found it. She came running to my desk, a huge smile on her face.

"You're the best!" she said, as her eyes began to fill with tears again.

I figured they were tears of joy, not fear. She asked me to bring it to Alan, as she really didn't want to see him if she didn't have to. My victory at finding the envelope made me happy to deliver it personally to the Prince of Pomposity.

"Here's the document, I said with success in my voice. I gave it to the property accountant, since it's his entity and it's from a bank. Being that it's such an important document I can't believe they didn't send it to your attention."

"Well, that's banks for you, glad you found it." Came his smug reply.

Alan turned back to his computer screen, an indication I was dismissed. He was such a piece of work, not even a "Thank you!" I really needed another job or more money!

By the end of the day I was exhausted. I spent my lunch hour going food shopping, so I wouldn't have to do it after work. The location of my office was another huge advantage of working for my ever demanding employer. Being in the heart of midtown Manhattan, gave me the opportunity to get tasks done during my lunch hour. Not to mention, I had the fastest commute one could imagine! One block walk to & from the subway in both directions, and a fifteen minute subway ride, and I was home. People commented on how lucky I was to have such a short commute in the city. I expressed that it went beyond luck.

When I relocated back to NYC after a six month stay in Stockholm, Sweden with my ex boyfriend, I was determined not to live in an outer borough. While I could have been in a nicer neighborhood for the same money, the short commute was worth the trade off.

I always said, pick a location as close to work as

possible. 25% of employees surveyed said they had quit a job due to the stress of a commute. Plus, I doubted I'd find an apartment as large as mine for the same money. So, I dealt with the neighborhood drug dealers and addicts, the Section 8 tenants in the building, and the jobless homies that took up residence out in front of my building most nights. When I got home the block was quiet. One of the only pluses with winter and rain, it kept the homies inside and the riff-raff off the street.

Of course Lulu was thrilled to see me. Before I could open the gate that kept her confined in the kitchen, she jumped up to kiss me. This welcome home never got old, her unconditional love constantly filled my heart. Her walk was quick and I was happy, it was bitterly cold! Back inside, I shivered as I undressed us, my finger tips were numb even though I had gloves on. I shook my head as I thought, we still have several more weeks to endure this….I poured a glass of wine. I had not heard from Mr. GQ all day. I was surprised to not have even received a morning text. Oh well, I reminded myself that unlike me, he was not a 9 to 6 employee. Self employed people really never stopped working, especially successful ones like him. I thought of texting, and decided to leave some space and make him wonder what I was up to. A nice hot shower, comfy lounge wear and some pre-prepared dinner goodies made for an easy night. I was in bed by 9:30.

Tuesday no call, no text. Wednesday the same, hmmm I wondered what was up with Mr. GQ.? Was his interest beginning to wane in the wasteland of the winter season?

Maybe he suffered from SAD as well, after all he was from the Caribbean. Thursday morning very early, just as I got out of bed, my phone chimed several times just after turning it on. Hot selfies of Mr. GQ filled my phone screen. He was truly a hottie, and he knew it! One was a summertime photo of him lounging with a cigar & a drink while sunbathing. What a package he was! I responded "Hottie"!!!!! And he requested photos from me. Comfortably settled in at work, I went to the ladies room. As I adjusted my outfit, a tunic style, dove gray mohair sweater with black leggings and thigh high black suede boots, made for a chic wintertime outfit. I decided my look was cool and a bit sexy. So, I took a selfie and sent it to him. A few minutes later my phone chimed.

His text read, "I love the look, very sexy! I can't wait to see you wearing those leggings in person!"

I giggled, as I texted, "Well, you will, I just bought a pair of faux leather leggings to wear to the game."

"Nicccce! What game are you going to?" he asked.

Huh? I thought, then I texted, "The game you're taking me to at the Barclays Center."

"Oh no Baby, that wasn't set in stone, I was just saying "maybe" we would go."

I couldn't believe what I was reading. He obviously forgot that he texted we had the tickets set. I gave him the benefit that he had forgotten, and I sent him a screenshot of his text to me saying we were all set for the Knick game court side. His response, "I'm a fucking idiot!" left me in a state of numbed confusion. Unclear about his comment, I texted saying, it was alright if he promised the tickets to a client or was taking a client, I was okay, there would be other games, but he provided no reply.

When I got in from walking Lulu, I promptly called Lori.

"Hi Baby Girl, how are you, how was your day?" she kindly inquired.

"Something is fishy with Mr. GQ, your suspicion may be right on point!"

I re-capped the events, the waning calls and texts and the correspondence from earlier at work.

"I knew it!!! Something told me he was too good

to be true! Yeah, he's a fucking idiot alright!"

"Well, I'm not throwing in the towel just yet. Maybe he had to jump into a meeting and couldn't give me a reasonable reply."

"Why are you making excuses for him? I think it's really obvious Baby Girl, he's not who you think he is!"

"Well, we don't know that for certain."

"I can't believe this is you talking! Why are you defending him?!"

"Oh man, Lor, you know how hard it is to meet a handsome, generous and successful guy today?!"

"Yes, I do! But, you have to guard your heart."

"This is really bumming me out! I thought for sure he was genuine. His belief in God & Jesus, telling me he prayed to meet an amazing woman like me. Buying me such an expensive gift, showering me with attention, I've been floating in this beautiful bubble of bliss, and now for reasons I don't understand, it has burst and I've landed hard on my butt, and feel like an ass!"

"I'm so sorry Baby girl, I know he's playing you."

"You're right. And, you know what? If he really is a player I already beat him at his game!"

"How so?"

"I never slept with him!"

"Maestro Of Manipulation"

Have you ever been played

By a maestro so grand

That he made you come

Just holding out his hand?

Did he tickle & play you

Like piano keys?

Till you screamed,

Yes, more, more please!

Did he place his Lips

Upon yours like he was

Playing A fine flute,

With lust so intense

You couldn't dispute.

Did he caress your body

Like the strings of a harp?

That made your heart

Quiver right from the start.

I had a maestro

Of my very own

Who tried to play me

Right out of my

Comfort zone.

He was smart so handsome

And very sexy,

To this day he'll Still text me.

His recited maneuvers

Were excellent

Emotional soothers.

I was falling deep into

His clever trap,

When my self made

Commitment came

Flooding back.

I held on to my

Flower that day,

When he didn't get his way,

I realized I was

Just another piece

He wanted to play.

Chapter 3: The Hurt

After I hung up with Lori, I had a glass of Chardonnay and replayed events in my mind.

If all he wanted was to sleep with me, why did he go to such extremes? I just didn't get it, and to bring God & Jesus into his act of seduction! As much as I was emotionally bruised, I knew how much worse I'd be feeling in this moment if I had slept with him!

Having been there before, I can personally say, there is no worse feeling than having fallen for and slept with a player! As women, when we believe a man is being sincere, we give our whole self to him, mind, heart and flower. Again, I clothed myself in the comfort of knowing I held on to my most precious gift from God. I had been so close to giving in! Man, and once he had entered my pleasure palace, there would be no erasing the memory of the moment.

I knew I would have given myself to him with all the desire, lust and passion that had been building in me for the past several years. He would have unleashed a vaginal volcano that would have erupted like molten lava when I climaxed. This would have created a connection to him as solid as concrete. I think I can state for most women, when a man makes us orgasm it intensifies the experience. Because most of the time our male partners are focused on themselves, their performance or they don't have the skill to take us to that mountain top. So while many times sex can be fun and hot for we women, rarely is it an experience that makes us cry out with passion, see fireworks and leave us desperate to see him again.

I decided to text Mr. GQ. "Hi Babe, hope you're having a good night. Just wanted to get clarity on our game night. Are we on or did you make plans with someone else. I'm totally cool either way. Please just let me know, so I can make plans to see friends if we aren't going." I didn't expect a response at that moment, knowing he went to bed super early. I really wanted him to explain himself. His comment truly threw me for a loop, and I wanted an honest answer. Even though I agreed with Lori, I wanted to see how this would play out. My head was reeling from the emotional rollercoaster ride he put me on.

Why did guys feel the need to play games? They created unnecessary drama by filling our heads with all kinds of sweet talk, only to pull the rug out from under us. Too tired to think any more I called it an early night.

The next morning there was no text from him.

Hmm, not a good sign. I got to work right on time, determined to stay focused on me, myself & I. There was plenty to keep me busy and keep my mind off Mr. GQ. Tax season was quickly approaching and the accounting department had tons of tax forms to be mailed out. Hundreds of envelopes filled my desk, leaving little room for me to handle other tasks. I made getting the envelopes stuffed and sealed for mail pick up was my main priority, the quicker I got rid of these tax mailings, the sooner I could resume working in my usually organized fashion.

As lunchtime rolled around, I began contemplating what to eat. I always ate a light lunch. I had learned the hard way that eating a heavy meal in the middle of the day, drained my energy and left me wanting to nap. I should have been born in Europe, where long and relaxing lunch breaks were the norm. I decided on a piece of spinach pie, light, filling and healthy. Walking southeast to my destination, I passed the store where I had purchased the bracelet for Mr. GQ. I began contemplating returning it. His lack of communication was making me back up big time. I'd see if he called or texted at some point in the day. If I didn't hear from him, I'd return it tomorrow for sure.

Back at work, I settled back into my tasks. When a guest arrived to see Henry.

"Hi Henry, there's a Mr. Stein here to see you regarding his closing."

"Okay Katie, please ask him to sit, I'll be out in a few minutes. I showed Mr. Stein to the sitting area.

"Wow, this is quite the set up, and a full view of Central Park, very impressive!"

This was often the reaction of many visitors. I was always asked if a photo could be taken. I always permitted it, but I asked them to be quick with the process. The owner loved to display his wealth, and though it was a show place, it was not furnished to my taste. The artwork was all abstract pieces, and one massive piece that hung near my desk was a huge black circle, it reminded me of the horror movie where the girl crawls out of a well. It was ugly, but worth a fortune, don't ask me why.

Henry greeted Mr. Stein, and asked if a conference room was available. I checked, and walked them to a room that overlooked the park. It was a view that never got old, season after season, it was God's canvas. As they settled into their chairs, I returned to my desk to wrap things up. It was getting late in the day and I wanted to leave promptly at 6:00. About forty minutes later Henry asked for my assistance with scanning the closing documents for Mr. Stein, and printing them out.

"Happy to help Henry, just email them to me and I'll get started." He thanked me graciously and returned to the conference room.

In a few minutes I had the document, it was over two hundred pages! I was glad I was getting a head start and sent it to the printer. When I went to retrieve it, the machine had jammed! "Damn it, so typical," I said out loud. I cleared the jam, went back to my desk and resent it. I explained to Henry and assured him I was handling it. Second time the machine ran out of paper!

"How's it coming along Katie?"

" Ughhhh! paper jam, then it ran out of paper, I decided to send it to a printer on the second floor."

"I'm sorry Katie, I appreciate all your help."

"I know Henry, I'll be right back."

Mission accomplished, I gave the documents to Mr. Stein & Henry. They both thanked me with true sincerity. It was 6:00 on the dot, I grabbed my bag, coat and said my good nights.

Happy to be home and relaxing, there was no word from Mr. GQ. What was his deal? I remembered that he was a Gemini, and I took into account the two personalities in the sign. I truly believed in Astrology, I found that it helped us to understand each other better, and most importantly not to take things too personally. If someone was cheap, they were cheap by nature, not just to certain people. Astrology had helped me navigate through so many situations with people in life, that it became a helpful tool in getting to someone's core.

Winter continued to be a wicked witch, the wind howled like a dingo in the desert. A perfect night for a rich soup. After showering and playing with Lu, I got down to preparing dinner. It was a simple, but delicious recipe of sautéed mushrooms, chicken stock, heavy cream and Marsala wine. After it started to thicken, Brie cheese and fresh thyme were the finishing touches. I gave it a taste, delish, I had out done myself! Mr. GQ had no idea what he was missing out on, his loss. Slices of a warm baguette with butter and a glass of Chardonnay completed my dinner.

The next morning still no word from Mr. GQ. I was annoyed, but thought, don't get angry, maybe something happened to him. I never assumed that in a city like NYC, everything was okay. Craziness happened everywhere all the time. I got ready for work and put the bracelet in my bag, should I decide to return it. I didn't know why I was hesitating to return it, I guess I was clinging to the hope that he might still be a good guy.

I arrived at the office to find a plain white envelope on my desk addressed to me. I hung up my coat, went to wash my hands and returning to my desk, I opened the envelope. Inside was a hundred dollar bill with a note that said, "A million thanks for all of your help."Mr. Stein. I was beyond surprised and grateful. It would definitely come in handy! I put the money in my wallet and saved the note in my calendar journal. I'd be sure to thank Henry as well. The morning flew by without any issues, and I was cruising through my work load. While my position did not require a degree in rocket science, it did demand the ability to work well under pressure, keep a track of checks for very large sums of money, handle the spontaneous requests of the owner, and be at the beck & call of over a hundred employees.

One day a guest was waiting for his contact to arrive. As he watched and listened to me work, he commented that I worked like an air traffic controller, as I simultaneously handled a variety of tasks. Colleagues constantly commended me for keeping the company humming. I was the glue that stopped things from coming undone.

"Good morning Katie."

"Good morning Henry, how are you?"

"Not sure yet, too early to tell. I never know what

insanity will be unleashed in this asylum."

I giggled and replied, "I hear you, my sentiments exactly. By the way, I appreciate the gift from Mr. Stein, I'd like to email him a note of thanks."

"Your assistance was stellar, we would have been here all night without your help. I'll send you his email address."

"Super! Thank you, and when you have some time today, I really need to talk to you.

"Sure Katie, no problem. I'll email you when I'm free."

Henry physically reminded me of Santa Claus, his demeanor was easy going and he was the person everyone went to with company issues, he was like a wise and patient grandfather. Henry was the designated, unofficial head of HR, because there was no HR department or even an office manager. Sound crazy for a company with over 100 employees and worth millions of dollars…repeat after me, insane asylum.

"I need more money, I cannot go on like this. I'm using almost $300 a month from my savings just to pay my rent." I got straight to the point with Henry.

"Katie, I don't even know how much you're

making."

When I told him, he raised his eyebrows and said, "And you live in Manhattan?! How are you surviving?"

"Like I said, augmenting my salary with my savings."

"Okay, let me discuss it at the Board meeting tomorrow. I think I can get you an extra

$10k, will that help?"

"It's a start Henry, thank you so much!"

"I see how hard you work and you've been acting as my assistant for months."

My desk was right down the main corridor from Henry's office, and he could literally hear and see everything I did.

"J.M. won't let me hire a new assistant, and he hates giving raises, but we have a strong case." Spoken like a true attorney. I left his office and thanked God for Henry.

"Hi there, I'd like to make a return please." I told the fashionably dressed store rep.

"Sure, please step over to the register and I'll be happy to help you."

"Thank you, I'm on my lunch break."

"I understand. May I ask the reason for the return?"

I wanted to say, "I've been a pawn in a player's game," but just said I changed my mind.

"Okay, I get it, just wanted to make sure you weren't disappointed with the quality."

We chatted about how cold it was, and that we still had to get through February. He commented that St. Valentine's Day was right around the corner. The thought put an extra damper on the return of the bracelet. Mr. GQ obviously would not be my Valentine.

The day had been commercialized to the point of it being a turn off for many people. In my opinion it was very sad because St. Valentine was a real priest that married young couples back in history, so that young men wouldn't be forced to go to war. If they were married they had a duty to stay and protect their wife and family. If more people knew the history they might embrace it more.

I walked quickly to the largest food chain in the area. They had a great selection of lunch items and prepared foods. I chose to have hummus, feta cheese and marinated olives. I grabbed a small pack of pita bread and went to the check out lines. The store carried some of the best food in the city, this location was always insanely busy! The checkout lines were so long, I was tempted to eat my lunch right on line! Fortunately, I picked a fast line and I was out and back at my desk right on time. I wasn't supposed to eat at my desk, but I was very discreet, kept my food out of sight and I never had anything pungent like tuna fish.

I had returned to a lot of work, primarily priority overnight shipments that were sometimes tedious in processing, either because of the lengthy addresses or international locations. I zipped through these as quickly as possible, they had to be dropped off by the end of day. I handled a few irate tenant calls, assisted vendors with check pickups, all while multitasking on other requests. I sure hoped Henry's pitch for my increase would go off without a hitch. I'd know tomorrow.

When I got home, I retrieved a number of pieces of mail, mostly bills of course. There was a Christmas card from my ex in Sweden. Claes, pronounced like Santa "Claus" and I had the good fortune of turning a relationship into a friendship. After more than six years in a long distance connection, he called it quits. I was devastated, but a prepaid ticket to Stockholm and his dad's ailing health, brought us back together. We reunited for several years, then I ended it. We eventually forgave each other, and focused on the outstanding things we had in common. Every few months we'd spend a couple of hours catching up on family, work and life in general. We always enjoyed our chats, and recognized our bond would last a lifetime. It was a simple card of a traditional Swedish Christmas tree, thin with long branches that held real flame lit candles. Amazingly, the tradition was still practiced by some Swedes.

The card simply read, "God Jul Et Gott Nytt Ar", Merry Christmas & Good New Year. I had studied and learned a bit of Swedish while living there for six months. The hard part of learning was that most Swedes speak fluent English and love to show off their ability to converse fluidly. Hence, I was speaking in my native tongue most of the time.

Spending a nice stretch of time in Sweden, Stockholm specifically, was truly one of my greatest life experiences. I absolutely loved the culture. The Swedes are a quiet and highly intelligent culture of people that enjoy minding their own business. Like my grandma would say, "Still waters run deep", meaning underestimating their ability to fiercely defend their country would be a foolish move for an enemy. Secretly, Sweden has some of the most advanced war armaments in the world, but remains a peaceful power unless provoked. Most Swedes are beautiful people, inside and out. I had always been attracted to blondes with blue eyes since I was a little girl. The old opposites attract concept fit me to the tee. As a Black woman I naturally stood out while living there, but I was looked at differently, because my looks were not that of the Africans that had settled there. I was often politely asked where I was from. My heritage was such a mix of Jamaican, Irish, Native American and Creole that I referred to myself as a mutt. I loved messing with the Census Bureau, I am forever an "Other" ….as many of us are.

When I got out of the shower, my phone chimed a text notice. Low and behold it was from Mr. GQ! "Hi Babe, how are you? I really need to see you! Can I see you tomorrow,

I want to give you your gift. Please let me know." That was it, no explanation of his going off the radar. There I was back on the emotional rollercoaster, lifted up by his text, but free falling with fear that this was his M.O. I was frozen by how to respond. I was so excited by his sudden reappearance, but still miffed about his leaving me hanging about the game, and if we were actually dating. This was not what I needed at the end of a long day. My response was, "Hi, long time no hear. I'm fine, hope you are too. I'll be in the office, text me tomorrow." I actually pondered repurchasing the bracelet.

Morning arrived with its intense winter chill. I clutched my duvet and I did my usual wake up routine. I dreaded getting out of bed, but this morning I had no time to linger. It was Board meeting day at the J.M. Group and it made for extra work and extra headaches. I had to organize pretty much everything for the meeting. I thought about my conversation with Henry and was thankful to know he'd be proposing my raise today.

It was a hard place to work, but colleagues like Henry, Mali and several others made it more bearable.

I made sure to look extra sharp that morning, as I mentioned the owner loved that I was a fashion plate, especially being the first face of the company. I wore a cherry red sweater dress with a silk & wool blended plaid scarf and black thigh high suede black boots. It was a combo that would keep me warm and look chic. When I got to the office the owner's son gave me a compliment immediately.

"Love the red Katie! Just the right color for a dreary winter day. You'll brighten everyone's day in that outfit."

Surprised by his overt compliment, he was usually very aloof and not a morning person, I thanked him with sincerity and got down to business.

Board meeting days were long and hectic! Everyone found that the day made it hard to get things accomplished, including the directors. Ten of them would be sequestered in a large boardroom for pretty much the entire day. JM sometimes ran late and the directors did as much work as they could before the meeting. When JM arrived it was my duty to round them all up and have them report to the conference room. I was once yelled at by a director for calling the assembly too early, saying JM hadn't arrived and it was 5 minutes before the scheduled time. I was not intimidated by him, he was disliked by many for his arrogance and snide comments. I firmly stated that JM had indeed arrived and had given me instructions to have the directors gather. As he walked away he nearly collided with JM, almost spilling his coffee. I smiled to myself, thinking that's what you get for acting like a bastard. He never approached me like that again.

It was also my responsibility to order lunch for them. This could have been a straightforward task, but noooo! Instead of ordering from one place and keeping it simple, they all chose to order from different places, which drove me nuts. There were times that I had to place orders to four different restaurants and coordinate the delivery times, so they could all be eating at the same time! There were days this was impossible, due to weather conditions and the locations of the eateries. I had to assist the office services lady with plating and serving. It was my longest day of the week.

By three o'clock I was starving, and I had not heard a peep from Mr. GQ! Again, I found myself feeling let down by his lack of follow up. I asked Mali to cover the phones while I went to get some lunch.

When I returned, the Board meeting had concluded, and as several of the directors passed my desk, they thanked me for their lunches and all my help. I suddenly remembered that Henry had planned to bring up my raise. No sooner did the thought come to my mind, when Henry called me to his office.

"Hi Henry, how was the meeting?"

"The usual, JM yelling about development deadlines not being met, but refusing to pay contractors and vendors, the usual nonsense. Anyway, I was able to get your increase approved, but not all at one shot. He agreed to $5,000 now. And the second $5,000 in a month. Is that okay with you?"

"Yes, I guess it has to be. It won't solve all my money issues, but it's a start. Thank you so much for making this happen."

"You're welcome, you deserve even more. I'm

going to tell Nellie to make sure to apply it to this pay period."

As I left his office I thanked God & Jesus for making this happen, ultimately, they were the true providers of blessings.

I never heard from Mr. GQ. What was his game?! To send me a text last night saying he needed to see me and then no communication at all?!!! I was again baffled by his blatant bad behavior. At this point I was beyond hurt, I was angry and fed up. After walking Lulu and taking a shower, I decided to text him. "Don't know what your game is, but I'm done! You tell me you "need" to see me and want to give me this mystery gift, yet, you don't communicate with me all day and leave me hanging like I don't have a life! I'm done, I'm returning the cross to you! So, give me an address to mail it to or I'm selling it and giving the money to the church." Within moments my phone chimed, his text read, "Nooo, you can't sell it, I gave it to you as a gift, and it's sacrilegious to sell a cross!"

I replied, "I Just don't get your disappearing act! I've done nothing to have you ghost me like this!" I was about to cry, but held my composure.

"You don't understand! I'm having health issues, my doctor discovered a hole in my heart!"

I was shocked and truly didn't know how to feel. Why hadn't he just come out and told me, instead of all this avoidance. I told him I was sorry to hear this news and would pray for him. I wouldn't sell the cross. This turning point in our connection led to this piece:

"Loving Myself First"

Even though I fell head

Over heels for you,

I couldn't give my

Flower to you

Too soon for you to taste,

The sweetness of my nectar

To feel my warm embrace

We agreed to take it slow

But, you became a no show

I love the fact that

We never slept together,

My head, heart and

Soul knew so much better.

As much as I quivered

To have your touch,

Your sudden absence

Would have been too much

For my heart to bear

Shedding continuous

Tear after tear.

So, in the end you went

From the guy with the most

To the biggest ghost.

I harbor no hurt, no pain,

Just glad I loved

Myself first once again.

Chapter 4: The Realization

I awoke in the middle of the night, tossing and turning. Thoughts about Mr. GQ running through my head. How did he go from being the best, to putting my head and heart through such a mercurial test? Once again, I found solace in the fact I never slept with him. True clarity came when I understood how in control I was that Christmas Eve night. Sex with him would have been on my terms not his. I pondered if this had been the reason he did an about face. When he realized that he couldn't buy his way into my bed, he decided I wasn't worth the time and more gifts. While my head and heart had some mending to do, my vagina had remained victorious in this mind boggling episode of my life. Furthermore, I realized that the cross would be my badge of honor, a constant reminder that God & Jesus came before anyone or anything. Ultimately following the "golden rules" led to a place of self love. I fell back into a very deep sleep.

In the morning Lori called.

"How are you Baby girl?" She chirped, in her adorable high pitched voice.

"I'm good, but I overslept!"

"Oh man, I know that feeling. You've been on my mind, what's up with the man?"

"Mr. GQ and I had a serious texting session. He told me he's been off the radar because

he found out he has a hole in his heart."

"Bullshit, I have a hole in my heart and it doesn't stop me from calling anybody! He's married, I'll go to my grave believing that. He tried to play you, thinking he could buy you with his wining, dining and gifts. He knows you're too classy to just fall into bed with a guy, so he tried extra hard to make you believe this was more than a conquest."

"I know you have a heart condition, but I've never known exactly what the issue is, how serious is it?"

"Well, I have to check in with my cardiologist for a regular check up, but that's it, trust me, he's being dramatic to cover his ass. His wife probably sensed something was up with him, so he had to do a 180."

"I still can't believe how hard I fell for him, and I'm still reeling. I hate feeling like this! Lori can you imagine how much worse I'd feel if I had slept with him? I'd really be beating myself up for playing the fool."

"I know Baby girl, I'm so proud of you for holding out, now you're the winner in his stupid game. Anyway, I got to get moving, work has been insane! I love you, stay strong, you'll get over this."

"I love you too, and thank you, I don't know what I'd do without you."

I was already starting to feel better, I thought about how fortunate I was to have an amazing girlfriend like Lori. Our friendship began at fourteen, freshman year in high school, and decades later we were still the best of friends and more like sisters. We shared everything about our lives without judgment. I saw the clock and thought, jeez I got to move it! I quickly walked Lu, jumped in the shower and I was out of the house in record time. I got to work about ten minutes late, and I was still earlier than a lot of other employees.

At lunch time I called my girlfriend Helen. A very intelligent and classy woman. Our 15 year friendship began while working at my previous firm. I trusted Helen with some of the most personal details of my life. She, like Lori, was one of my dearest friends. I valued her and I knew Helen valued me too. She was working at a miserable architectural firm. They ran her ragged and barely acknowledged her willingness to go above and beyond. I prayed she'd find a better job soon.

"I realize it's over with Mr. GQ, this isn't going anywhere."

"I can't believe what I'm hearing, when did all of this start?"

"You've been so busy at that psych ward of an office you're working at, and so exhausted when you get home, I didn't want to beleaguer you with the delusional episodes of this dating situation."

"You know you can always call me."

"I know my dear friend, I'm blessed to have you."

I shared all the details with her, the back to back broken Saturday night plans, the basketball game debacle, and his promise to deliver the mystery gift that I no longer believed existed. Even how I had been so beside myself that I was going to return the cross or sell it.

"Wow! Katie I'm so sorry! I thought for sure he was genuine. I have to say, I'm really glad you weren't intimate with him, you'd be feeling worse."

My dear friend knew me well. She had been there through both of my horrendous break ups. Always providing a strong shoulder to cry on, and always giving sound advice. How I loved and cherished my girlfriends! It's been said, "Friends are the family you choose" I agreed and I had chosen wisely. I didn't have much of an appetite, so I chose to just run a few errands. Once again, the convenience of working in midtown Manhattan was a true blessing. Poor Helen was working all the way downtown in the financial district. The streets were narrow and crowded at lunchtime, and dark and deserted at night. There were far fewer eateries, places to shop and her commute was hellacious. She initially thought I was crazy to take the position at J.M. Group.

"Katie, how are you going to live on that money?! I think you should wait for something else to come along."

"Believe me, I hear you, but I'm thinking, location, location, location. I can run home at lunchtime if necessary to feed and walk Lu. Not to mention my commute will only be two subway stops, I'll make it home in no time."

She now applauded my decision. Wow, I had forgotten to tell her about my raise. I was so consumed with the sad reality that Mr. GQ was not my soulmate, that I had completely forgotten to share my good news. Relationship drama can really mess with our minds, cause depression and anxiety. I was not going any further down that path.

One of my errands was getting flowers for Henry.

I had inquired of Mara, whether he would prefer luxury chocolates or flowers.

"Definitely flowers, he has a real affinity for nature."

"Great, flowers it will be."

I purchased a lovely bunch of roses the color of a sunset. Yellow gave way to orange that blended into a reddish hue, truly gorgeous. I asked for a small card. I picked up some egg salad and healthy chips and headed back to work. At my desk, I kept the flowers hidden, and wrote out my note of thanks to Henry as I noshed on my lunch. I addressed several tasks and before I knew it was after 5:00. I knocked on Henry's office door.

"Come on in Katie."

"Thanks Henry. These are for you. I can't express how much your help means to me."

"Katie, you really didn't have to, their beautiful. I wish I could have gotten you more and sooner, but I'm glad JM approved it at all."

"I know, and I always try to show him my commitment to the firm."

"Well, you do and other directors notice your commitment too." We said our "good nights" and I bundled up to face the cold night air.

When I arrived at home, I met my girlfriend and neighbor, Tindu, in our lobby.

"Hey Katie, what' up girl? You lookin' fly in that fabulous fur!"

"Hi Tindu, thank you honey, you know how I hate the winter, got to stay as warm as possible." I gave her a big hug.

"You know I hear that, shit I can't stand anything below 75 degrees."

Tindu and I had become fast friends. Her physical characteristics reminded me of the singer, Macy Gray from back in the day, militant, but with a flair of femininity. Born and raised in Harlem, she was "a round the way girl", street savvy with a quick wit and she didn't take any shit! She was the daughter of a smart and tough woman, and as the saying goes, "the apple doesn't fall far from the tree." Tindu cursed unapologetically like a pissed off truck driver. Her highly intelligent comments on anything from relationships, to politics, were always peppered with the most definitive expletives. Our first meeting occurred on a summer evening. I had just returned home from work and I was exhausted. As I started to unwind, I heard a woman talking really loud to several other women. When I looked out my bedroom window, I saw Tindu holding court in the front of the building.

"Excuse me ladies, would you please lower your voices? I just got home from work and I have a terrible headache."

I made certain to be respectful in my request, I wasn't trying to get into an altercation. Tindu gave me the once over and said, "Sure, so sorry darling' we'll keep it down, no problem."

"Thank you so much, it's been a long day." As I walked away, she kindly said,

"Take care and feel better."

I thanked her, and felt a sense of relief that she had been understanding and not offended. A few weeks later we ran into each other coming in from work. We had a conversation about the rapid growth of gentrification in the neighborhood. Much to my surprise and pleasure, Tindu was embracing the change too.

Though Tindu was completely connected to her Black heritage, unlike myself, her open mindedness and natural curiosity made her willing to accept people as they were.

"What's been going on Katie? How's that hottie you been seeing?"

"Hottie, was a flash in the pan!"

"What you mean by that?"

"It's a long story, you free for a glass of wine?"

"You know it! Let me get out of my work outfit and I'll come down in a little while."

"Sounds perfect."

Tindu arrived about 45 minutes later, this had given me the chance to walk Lu, shower and change into warm loungewear. When I opened the door, she was there with a bottle of wine wearing a graphic hoodie and leggings, T always looked cool even in hangout garb. I shared the entire saga with Tindu, as she played with Lu, but listened intently.

She took a sip of wine and said, "Girrrrrllll, I'm glad you played it the way you did! These motherfuckers always be playing games. Lori's right, I bet he is fuckin married and thought he could get some nice classy pussy on the side."

"I know T, I'm just so glad I took control of the situation. I guess I've finally learned after playing the fool too many times before. We women long for love so bad, that we fall into bed and then realize we been had! This is a new beginning for me, it has set a precedent for how I'll handle guys going forward."

"I'm proud of you girl, some women never wake up, they just keep put pussy out there thinking it gonna keep him, shit it takes more than a wet pussy to keep a man these days."

If there was anyone I knew that could speak her mind, it was Tindu. She stayed for dinner, thankful for the invite. T loved good food, but she did not cook, she was never taught and couldn't get into it. She existed on cereal, sandwiches and the occasional takeout from the local Chinese place. She devoured every morsel and complimented me on the meal. I told her about how I negotiated my raise and how much it would help my financial situation.

"Katie that's awesome, congrats Darling, you deserve it, you bust your butt at that company."

As the reality of another work day loomed ahead of us, we hugged goodnight and Tindu giggled with glee from Lulu's goodnight kisses.

Chapter 5: The Acceptance

Days turned into weeks, and slowly but surely Mr. GQ was becoming more of a distant memory. The morning calls and texts had ceased, and my life began to return to the normalcy I once knew. Occasionally, someone from his company would come to the office to pick up a check. One day it was one of his brothers, the resemblance was too striking.

"How's your brother doing?" I casually inquired.

"He's good, working hard, he lives at the gym, he's always worried about his weight, you know he used to be over three hundred pounds! Don't tell him I told you!"

"Wow, I had no idea. No worries, the secret is safe with me."

He signed for the check and waved goodbye. So, at some point Mr. GQ had been the size of a house and not such a hottie. That past insecurity could account for his behavior. Even though he had lost the weight, he still carried that baggage and more.

That evening I allowed myself time to truly relax

and unwind. As I sipped a delicious glass of one of my favorite wines, I toasted myself for my victories in my personal and business life. This was going to be the year I focused on me. This ephemeral relationship had taught me more in a few months than I had learned in relationships that had lasted years. I began to realize how important it is to ask questions when dating someone, and to really analyze their responses.

We are so often caught up in how good looking the guy is, or his successful lifestyle, that we don't actually LISTEN to what he is saying and sharing.

I sat in a place of reflection, I thought back on the conversation with Mr. GQ on Christmas Day. The animosity with which he spoke about his relationship with his mother came flooding back to me. He had shared that in a violent moment, with a criminal she had been spending time with, she was forced to call the police. When they arrived they arrested the guy. As he and his little brothers stood by and watched, the officers asked her, "Would you like us to take the boys and put them in a home?" Her response was, "Yes, take them." Mr. GQ had flown into a rage, refusing to go. He contacted his uncle, who saved him and his brothers from a life of abandonment and poverty. As I played out the scene in my mind, I cannot imagine the amount of hurt and fear that he would have been experiencing at that very young age, I think he said he was about ten. To have his own mother be willing to give him and his brothers up, to complete strangers, right in front of his face, must have felt like a cannon ball hitting his gut. I have to believe the emotional trauma left a lifetime wound. How could he ever really love or trust a woman?! Unless he really took the time to reflect, confront and forgive his mother, he would carry that massive cannonball of baggage with him forever.

My heart broke for him.

Arriving at this place of compassion, brought my heart to a lighter place. I no longer felt hurt or rejected, I had reached a point of understanding that lifted me to another realm. His behavior toward me had nothing to do with me, it was how he chose to navigate his life. I realized that it only took learning about one major chapter in someone's life, to reveal so much about them, and prevent one from being the recipient of tremendous disappointment and heartbreak. This had been the "Red Flag" that I had chosen to see as a "Pink Flag" because I wanted a relationship with him so much.

The following morning I awoke feeling lighter and happier than I had in ages. The mental deep drive I took to rchash thc past couple of months with Mr. GQ, did my mind and heart a world of good. As I said my prayers, I began to cry tears of joy because I could feel the love of God and Jesus surrounding me, reassuring me that all would be fine. It's so important to take time to be alone. It is in moments of solitude that we often find our greatest moments of clarity. As I turned on the lamp, pulled on my robe and slipped into my warm and comfy slippers, I sensed it was going to be a super day!

Given the day was forecasted to be sunny, but blustery, I chose to wear a light gray dress of angora and wool with a matching gray ruffled wrap held in place by a beautiful starfish brooch. The brooch was a gift and one of my favorite pieces of jewelry. A few years before, I had received a generic gift card from a dear colleague as a get well gift after a surgical procedure. I wanted to get something special that would always remind me of her thoughtfulness. When I showed her the brooch, she thought it was gorgeous and she was thrilled that I had found something so lovely.

When I arrived at my office building, I was met with a hiccup. As I approached the elevator bank, a number of colleagues and tenants stood staring at the elevator display screen, it was black. Apparently, all six elevators that went to the upper floors were not functioning! Holy smokes! We stared at each other dumbfounded. Just then JM arrived, as the owner of the entire building, the tenants and company employees looked to him   for a solution. Within seconds he ordered us to the other elevator bank. These elevators would take us to the 14th floor, but then we would have to walk all the way up to the 26th floor! Why was this the day I chose to wear high heeled boots?! Oh man, my tootsies would be toast by the time I got to my desk!

By the time we reached the 20th floor, people were starting to feel the burn in their legs. Fortunately, I stayed on a regular fitness routine that kept me in good shape. JM tried the stairwell door, it was locked. Certain floors had no re- entry access for fire safety reasons. I heard a voice say "No way!" Then JM said, "We have to walk back down."

I said, "Wait, let me call the security desk, they can call the tenant on this floor and have them give us access." I pulled out my cell and dialed the number from memory.

"Hi John, it's Katie from J.M. Group, we're stuck in the stairwell on 20, can you get the tenant to let us in? Super! Thanks a lot!" JM ignored this and started walking back down, I shook my head, what was he thinking. In moments the stairwell door was opened by a pretty young woman. JM did an about face and joined the rest of us for our final journey up the stairs.

One of my favorite colleagues, Patricia said, "Man Katie, that was really quick thinking!

There was no way I was walking back down those stairs! Just another reason you deserve that raise, you're a smart woman!"

"Awww, thanks Pat, it takes one to know one!"

We high fived and made our way to our desks. I sat with a sigh of relief and removed my boots. I slipped on a comfy pair of flats I always kept under my desk. I went to the kitchen, got a glass of ice for my morning tonic and returned to my desk to begin my day. Deliveries of office and kitchen supplies arrived, and as I transferred the boxes from the elevator area to inside the office, the freight elevator door suddenly opened, startling me! A very handsome young delivery guy emerged from the elevator holding several overnight envelopes.

"Good morning, he said, how are you today?"

"Good morning, I'm well thanks, how are you?" I replied

"Pretty good, you know hustlin hard."

He was a Latino cutie, with dark almond eyes and a nice complexion.

He handed me the envelopes, and as I signed for them, I could feel him staring at me. I looked at him and said, "Is everything okay?"

"Yeah, but can I ask you something?"

"Sure, what's up?"

"Are those really your eyes?"

It was a question that was often asked with hesitation. Dark with a rim of light blue, the color of my eyes surprised many. People often assumed I was wearing contacts.

"Yes, they are my eyes, not contacts."

"Damn woman, they're mesmerizing! Let me go before I get myself in trouble!"

Blushing, I thanked him as he smiled and got on the elevator. That was a super compliment from a very young buck! He couldn't be more than twenty-three!

As I prepared to deliver the overnight envelopes, JM walked in.

"Good morning Katie, please have Cindy get me a large skim milk latte."

"Good morning JM, of course, I'll ask her to get it immediately."

"Thank you, and please tell building maintenance, elevator number five needs to be wiped down, the walls are covered with fingerprints."

"Yes sir, I'll contact them promptly."

JM was a stickler for cleanliness and organization. Fortunately, those habits were part of my DNA and I knew he liked that about me. I addressed his requests before getting sidetracked. I had just returned to my desk, when I got a call from the security desk.

"Hi Katie, there's a guest here to see Hakim and you, he said he has a meeting."

"Okay Steven, you can send him up."

Hmmm, who would be here to see Hakim and me? Hakim was the head of construction.

Just then Mr. GQ walked in carrying a package wrapped in brown paper.

"Good morning, good morning!"

"Good morning to you too! This is a surprise!" I replied

"And this is for you, long overdue."

I thanked him and took the package. It was fairly large and square like a piece of artwork, I tried to imagine what it could be. With no space at my desk, I placed it in the coat closet.

"How are you, it's been awhile." I casually stated.

"I'm okay, well not really. Business has been a

bitch, a lot of deals have been put on

hold. It's stressing me out."

"Sorry to hear, I know JM has been all over the construction team to get projects finished."

"Yeah, that's why I'm here to meet with Hakim, I'm not looking forward to this meeting.

Do you have any tea and maybe lemon? My throat is really bothering me."

"Tea yes, and I can add some of my own lemon tonic and honey, sound good?"

"Awesome, thank you."

As I made my way to the pantry, I felt very proud of myself, I was cool, calm and collected. All the reflecting and mental rehashing had done me a world of good. My interlude with Mr. GQ was now a distant memory.

I returned with the mug of tea and the promised lemon and honey. He took a sip and sighed. "I really appreciate this, it's very good, I needed it."

"My pleasure. I'll call Hakim for you now."

"That's okay, I'm early. I wanted to mentally prep for this meeting. I'm concerned he's going to cut the budget for the job, and if he docs, it's going to create a domino effect of issues."

"Wow, sounds like a lot. But, you know you must maintain a positive attitude, if you fear a negative outcome, you can actually manifest it, and that's the last thing you want."

"You're right, and a wise woman."

"Thank you, I try to be, but I'm not always. We're all only human."

"So, what have you been up to?" He inquired.

"Just dealing with life and getting through the winter." "You're still here, are things better?"

"No, but I did negotiate a raise."

"Super, congrats! I told you JM values you."

Just then Mali arrived. She greeted us as she hung her coat and settled in at her desk.

"I've got to go deliver these packages. Mali will call Hakim for you when you're ready. Good luck with your meeting, I'm sure things will work out."

"I appreciate that."

"I have an appointment soon, so I'll probably be gone when you're ready to leave. So, feel better and stay strong."

"Your words mean a lot, thank you."

I made my way down to the second floor of the office. I delivered the overnight envelopes and caught up with a few colleagues I didn't get to see often. By the time I returned, Mr. GQ was in a conference room with Hakim. Things appeared to be going well, Hakim was JM's pit bull and he had no qualms about screaming at construction vendors. I had witnessed many a shouting match and it was never a pretty sight.

When I returned from my appointment Mr. GQ was gone. I was so happy at the way I had interacted with him, I was sincere and sympathetic. Mali asked how I was doing.

"I'm fine, no butterflies and no regrets." I told her.

"I'm glad Katie, I know you really liked him. I was hoping things would have worked out for you guys."

"Thanks girl, I know. But, he has some serious baggage that he has got to unload, and

I'm sure he's still married."

"You're truly a strong woman and I admire how you handled the whole situation. So many women want to turn things into a drama, and what good does it do!"

"I hear you and that's so not my style."

The rest of the day was an onslaught of nonstop phone calls, check pickups, messenger requests and emails. By the end of the day Mali and I were pooped, and ready to hit the road. Getting our coats out of the closet, she spotted the package.

"What's that?" She asked.

"Oh, I almost forgot, it's the mystery Christmas gift from Mr. GQ."

"Wow, wonder what it is?"

"Yup, me too. I'm not happy about schlepping it on the train."

As luck would have it the train Mali and I got on was fairly empty and I had no issues navigating my package. Once at home, I carefully propped it against the living room wall, and took Lulu for her walk. Back inside and unbundled, Lulu followed me over to the package. I simply could not imagine what he had gifted me. I removed the paper to reveal a framed collage of photos I had shared with Mr. GQ. Pictures of my mom, sister and me, a baby photo I had shared upon his request, and a few more nice photos. It was indeed a very thoughtful gift. It didn't really work with my decor, so I put it in the bedroom. I sent him a quick text of thanks, and started thinking about dinner.

A roast beef sandwich with caramelized red onions, mushrooms and blue cheese on a brioche bun was the perfect way to end a long day. Homemade sweet potato fries and a glass of Cabernet completed my meal. I said grace as always, so grateful for my blessings. I loved my own company and I was thankful that I did, so many people can't be alone. They would rather be with people they don't like, than to be alone. I truly felt sorry for people like that. I gave Lulu a few tiny pieces of roast beef as I finished up my dinner. I washed the dishes, blew out the candles I had lit and retired to bed.

I woke up realizing it was Friday! Yay!!! The mornings were beginning to brighten a little earlier everyday, and that brightened my mood. Prayers said, bed made and dressed to walk Lu, I got my day started. It was a sunny morning and as I passed neighbors, I wished them a "Good morning & Happy Friday." Showered, hair and makeup completed, I quickly dressed in black leggings, a white long sleeve shirt, a cashmere cardigan and leather riding boots. I gave Lu her breakfast and dashed out the door. I picked up a blueberry muffin and fruit salad for breakfast. The office was very quiet when I arrived, hopefully it would remain that way.

The handsome young Latino courier arrived again, and I learned his name was Manny. He had just inherited the route from a driver who retired. He handed me several envelopes and said, "It's nice to see you again and I hope you have a terrific weekend."

"Thank you, you too. Looks like we'll be seeing each other regularly."

"Yes, seeing you is definitely a perk."

He winked and left. Being hit on by a 23 year old was definitely a great way to start the weekend. Suddenly my phone was ringing, as I picked it up, I saw that it was Mr. GQ.

"Good morning" I answered.

"Good morning Sunshine! Happy Friday!"

"Happy Friday to you too! To what do I have the pleasure of this call?"

"I just had to say thank you for your words of encouragement yesterday. The meeting went very well."

"Oh good, I'm so happy for you."

"I also want to thank you for putting up with my nonsense, I'm sorry."

"I appreciate your apology. After reflecting on some of what you shared of your past, especially your relationship with your mother, I began to realize that you have a lot of emotional things that you still need to rectify. So, that being said, I'm glad that we can move forward as friends."

"You're right, thank you for that and for willing to be my friend."

He wished me a good weekend and said he'd stay in touch. I smiled as I hung up, thinking all's well that ends well.

I realized in the end that by not being intimate with Mr. GQ that night, I was putting myself first. Which tied right back to my connection with God & Jesus. When They are truly present in our lives we make different decisions, decisions that lead to a happier and peaceful relationship with one's highest self. I once got a fortune cookie quote that I carried for years, it said, "Your First Love & Last Love Should Be Self Love.".....

"Pearl of Wisdom"

She kept the secrets of

Her life sealed

Like an oyster shell.

So gritty were some

That she would Never tell.

But, one day she

Took all the debris

Of her life,

And like a surgeon

She cut into her

Past with a mental knife.

Analyzing each moment

Like a grain of sand

Studying and remembering

So she would always understand,

That every experience

Gathered all up

Flowing from life's cup

Reminded her not to ever give up

All she had learned

An all she had gained

Became a pearl of wisdom

That would lead her

To a glorious kingdom

Of self-love

As ordained by

God & Jesus above.

Special Thanks

I would like to thank:

God & Jesus Christ for giving me my spiritual compass.

Claudia Moran, my mother for loving me & giving me an invaluable education. Christel Moran, my sister, who's always there. Ron Moran-Holzmann, amazing friend who kept telling me what a great writer I am.

Frederick Johnson, dearest friend & proofreader. Helen Halis, dearest friend & confident. Kai Mueller, dear friend, who also encouraged me to write. Loriana Ferrari, childhood girlfriend a.k.a partner in crime. Shaun Thompson, dearest friend & supporter. Patricia Dease, dear friend and supporter. And Tindu Memminger, dearest friend & supporter. If you didn't make the list, please know I love you dearly and had to stop before the list became longer than the book!

God & Jesus' blessings!

Love, Katie

About the Author

Katie Slade was raised in the Chelsea area of Manhattan. She attended Parochial schools her entire life, which cemented an excellent educational & spiritual foundation. As a women empowerment mentor, it is her desire to help as women as possible learn to respect, value and love themselves unconditionally.

Through her "Love Yourself More" workshop, she assists women by focusing on building a loving relationship with themselves. She has traveled extensively within the U.S. the Caribbean, England, France, Spain and lived in Sweden. Katie's love of writing re-emerged during the pandemic, and she has a second book on the way.

She now spends most of her time in Mexico with her Yorkshire terrier, Lulu. She can be contacted via: kslayit@gmail.com - kslayit.website - slayitbykslade on IG - "The Katie Slade Show" on YouTube. Get her t-shirt via Etsy at kslayit.com.

The End.

Look for Katie's sequel "The Virtuous Vagina: How To Leave Lust In The Dust & Find Clarity Through Chastity."

Get ready for another rollercoaster ride, as Katie navigates dinner invites, propositions for hook ups and relationships from a plethora of hot & sexy men who all have an agenda! Join her on this real life adventure of more twists and turns, but definitely more highs than lows!

www.ingramcontent.com/pod-product-compliance
Lightning Source LLC
Chambersburg PA
CBHW061138160726
48006CB00038B/2137